# reading R<sub>x</sub>:

## better teachers
## better supervisors
## better programs –

Joseph S. Nemeth, *Editor*
Bowling Green State University

International Reading Association
800 Barksdale Road    Newark, Delaware 19711

156021

372.4
P 2873

# INTERNATIONAL READING ASSOCIATION

Copyright 1975 by the
International Reading Association, Inc.
Library of Congress Cataloging in Publication Data
Main entry under title:

Reading Rx : better teachers, better supervisors,
better programs.

Includes bibliographies.
1. Reading—Addresses, essays, lectures.
I. Nemeth, Joseph S.
LB1050.R425    428'.4    75-14103
ISBN 0-87207-454-4

# CONTENTS

# A BACKWARD GLANCE—A FORWARD LOOK

Only a few hundred years ago it was taken for granted that eminent scholars would keep their secrets to themselves. Problems they shared generously—but not solutions. The latter would have meant a loss of personal power in a competitive field. Today, thanks to the generosity of people like Joseph Nemeth and the authors whose work he has compiled and edited, we can learn answers as well as questions.

No matter what your role in teacher education or program development, you will find the ideas in this volume useful and provocative. All that you need to do is to approach the book with an attitude of inquiry prompted by the conviction that reading is a moving field in which all is not yet known, and that knowledge of new developments is essential even to one who would wish only to maintain his relative position. As in *Alice in Wonderland,* one must run to stand still.

I have just returned from another great Annual Convention of the International Reading Association, impressed again with the impossibility of keeping up with all aspects of the field in its breadth, its depth, and its variety; further convinced by the fact that I physically could not attend every session of all the simultaneous strands which invited my attention.

Luckily, the book is not obsolete in our society. You can choose a time to devour all of this one and, without fear of obesity, gain stature in your chosen field. Alice did the same thing, you will remember, by drinking from a bottle; but I suggest you try this more heady fare. It will take you forward as well as upward.

Bon voyage! Bon appétit!

Constance M. McCullough, *President*
International Reading Association
1974-1975

# INTRODUCTION

When are reading teachers, supervisors, or consultants too old to teach? Certainly not when they reach the biblical threescore and ten. Teachers and others are too old to teach when

- the cloak of complacency prevents them from taking time to read,
- the fire of learning has died within,
- the acceptance of new ideas and challenges is refused,
- passive thoughts take over.

Those are some of the things which make teachers age quickly and make them "old" professionally. It can happen at any age— twenty-eight, forty-eight, eighty-eight. Who is too old to learn is too old to teach.

And in part, how much a teacher learns and continues to learn is directly proportional to the quantity and quality of his pre- and inservice education. Pre- and inservice trainers of teachers understand this. They realize that a teacher's classroom performance will be directly related to how he feels about his training and himself. Because it is critically·important to education that teachers learn and continue to learn, the good teacher trainer must rethink and improve his methods continually.

This volume is largely directed toward the improvement of teacher education. It is divided into three parts. The first two parts wrestle directly with current issues and offer suggestions for the improvement of teacher education. Part three specifically treats some of the reading programs which the teacher implements as a consequence of his training.

Lack of real interest, desire, and drive is the robber of teacher growth, maturity, and longevity. Without them, a teacher dies at twenty-eight, forty-eight, or eighty-eight. With them, any teacher can live a full teaching age, regardless of the calendar. It is hoped that this volume will make a contribution toward that end.

JSN

The International Reading Association
attempts, through its publications, to provide a forum for a wide spectrum of opinion
on reading. This policy permits divergent
viewpoints without assuming the endorse-
ment of the Association.

# teacher training:
## preservice and inservice

"My primary duty as a teacher's aide is to teach . . .
freeing the teachers to handle tickets, supervise
the lunchroom, monitor halls, collect money, etc."

# COMPETENCY BASED READING PREPARATION FOR SECONDARY TEACHERS

*Howard G. Getz*
*and*
*Larry D. Kennedy*
*Illinois State University*

For many years, educators have recognized the necessity for providing continued reading instruction for secondary level students. Unfortunately, teacher education institutions have not always been as responsive as they might have been to this need. Historically, teacher education institutions have attempted to provide secondary level preservice teachers with the knowledge and skills related to helping their secondary students with reading problems by providing either short units within an existing methods course or by offering a separate course.

## Certification Requirements

At Illinois State University, all undergraduates in the secondary school teacher education program are required for certification to take a two-credit-hour course designed to familiarize them with the scope and nature of secondary level reading problems. Traditionally, this two-hour course, Secondary School Reading, has been taught as a separate course by a member of the reading area of the department of education. Over several years, however, the reading area faculty has reorganized the content and skills of Secondary School Reading to facilitate the movement of secondary level reading instruction from a course-centered structure to a teaching-learning structure that is competency based.

## Theoretical Base

The current secondary school reading program is designed specifically as a competency based program. Success in the program is based upon individual attainment of proficiency over specified instructional objectives in the reading area. This competency based program is based upon the General Model of Instruction. The General Model of Instruction is a procedural guide for designing and conducting instruction. The major philosophical assumption of the GMI is that the goal of instruction is to maximize the efficiency with which all students achieve specified instructional objectives. The model is based upon a technology of instruction developed over the past several years from research and development work in experimental psychology, military training, and programed instruction. The two major functions of the model are 1) to guide instructional designers and teachers through the major steps in designing and carrying out instruction, and 2) to provide an overall structure with which to view and study the instructional process (1).

## Overview of the Program

The competency based program in reading is only one element in the entire competency based program required of preservice secondary school teachers at Illinois State University. The sequence (the entire program is called the Professional Sequence), consisting of eleven hours of course work, also includes four hours of credit in a methods course, a two-hour background course in education, and a three-hour course in educational psychology. Thus, if a student enrolled in the secondary program before it moved to its present structure, he would have taken the following courses:

| | |
|---|---|
| Secondary School Reading | 2 hours |
| Secondary Education | 4 hours |
| American Public Education | 2 hours |
| Educational Psychology | 3 hours |

The sequence is made up of approximately eighty instructional packages which are described in some detail in a subsequent section. The basic premises of the sequence include the following: 1) students should be allowed to work at their own pace; 2) students should not be required to attend any classes unless they so desire or unless they call for the class themselves; 3) when a student finishes a package, he should be able to take a test without having to wait for others; 4) material should be so structured that information is not repeated unless the repetition is necessary to reinforce knowledge; 5) required material should be that portion of total material the faculty agrees is a necessary part of the teacher education program; and 6) students should reach a proficiency level that would normally be equivalent to a *B* grade before they are given credit for any particular package.

At the beginning of the semester, students meet en masse for four hours to receive an introduction to the sequence and to fill out the necessary forms. The students are shown a series of slides which provides them with an overview of the entire sequence. Students are then assigned to a five-member instructional team made up of one specialist in the area of educational psychology, three specialists in secondary methods and background, and one specialist in the reading area.

Following the initial meetings, the faculty provide nonrequired classes on a rotating basis four days per week. Faculty are available for individual instruction or counseling for at least eight hours per week in addition to regular office hours.

## Learning Package Components

Eighty instructional packages are published in *The Professional Sequence Guide* and are composed of the following elements:

> Instructional Objectives
> Questions to be Answered
> Learning Activities—Required
> Learning Activities—Optional
> Evaluation.

Each package is given a particular number (reading packages are numbered 0301 through 0319) and assigned a number of merits equal to the approximate number of hours required to complete that package.

## Instructional Objectives

The instructional objectives constitute the core of the learning packages. These objectives are stated in behavioral terms and are intended to provide the student with a precise knowledge of what is expected of him. The instructional objectives specify what the student must do as he works on the objective and the level of proficiency required for him to complete the objective successfully. Every element following in the learning package must be constructed to maximize the potential of the student to complete the objective. In brief, the instructional objective dictates the selection of study questions, learning activities, and the final evaluation. Sample instructional objectives include the following:

> Given information about test administration and evaluation, the student will be able to administer to at least one other student and to evaluate the results of either the Nelson-Denny or the Stanford Achievement Test: Reading. The student will demonstrate his proficiency by completing an evaluation form and submitting it for Pass/No Pass scoring.

Given materials related to aids to reading in the content fields, the student will be able to identify the nature and the function of Assignment-Readiness, SQ3R Study Procedures, and Reading-Study Skills by achieving 80 percent accuracy on an objective test over the material.

## Questions to be Answered

Each instructional objective is followed by a section identified as *Questions to be Answered*. The purpose of this section is to guide the student through the learning activities so that he can obtain the information that will facilitate his meeting the objective. This section directs the student's attention in his reading of professional articles to those points that are relevant to the attainment of the objective. If the learning activities contain videotapes, audiotapes, or tape-slides, questions are also asked to guide the acquisition of this knowledge. In brief, this section directs the student's attention toward the information he must know. Sample questions include:

- What are the basic characteristics of the teaching of the language experience approach to reading?
- In what ways are the approaches to reading related to reading at the secondary school level;
- What standardized tests are available to measure the reading ability of secondary school students?
- Are there differences in what standardized reading tests measure?

## Learning Activities—Required

Learning Activities—Required is designed to list readings, audiovisual materials, or exercises that will specifically help the student reach the instructional objective. Since few books contain *all* of the materials students must become acquainted with in the area of secondary school reading, the students are not required to purchase one text book to complete their nineteen objective packages. Instead, multiple copies of many books are made available in the library so students can read the required articles at leisure. Looseleaf materials are also kept on file in the library to help the students through the learning activities.

When the material for the learning activity is available through a tape, a tape-slide, or a filmstrip, a typescript of the tape is also made available to the student so that he may choose the sensory approach most satisfactory to his style of learning.

The audiovisual materials are made available in a room called the learning lab, a converted language laboratory. Here a student goes to a carrel, punches in his social security number and the number of the program desired (e.g., #24, "Standardized Reading Tests: Basic Information"), waits for the program to be duplicated for his own use, and then has complete control of the program. The controls allow him to stop the program and back it up if it is moving too quickly or to push the fast forward button if it is moving too slowly. In any case, he has complete control and is not governed by any other student's progress. This random access system was developed by AMPEX, and Illinois State University was the first university to use the system for a teacher education program.

Some examples of required learning activities follow:

1.  Read the article by Hafner, Lawrence E., "The Uses of Reading and the Need for Reading Instruction," in *Improving Reading in Secondary Schools*, pp. 2-13. In the North Reserve Room of Milner Library.

2.  Listen to the audiotape "Assessment of Reading Readiness" in the Learning Lab, Edwards Hall 201.
    OR
    Read the typescript under the same title in the Professional Sequence file in the North Reserve Room.

3.  Observe the videotape on "The Analysis of Reading Performance" in the Learning Lab, Edwards Hall 201.

## Learning Activities—Optional

The materials presented in this section are quite similar to those in the previous section. The main difference is that when students move through the required materials and find some difficulty in learning from that presentation, some optional materials must be made available. These optional materials either present the information in a different way or provide new information that will eventually lead to the same goal. Examples of optional learning activities follow the same format as those of the required activities listed above.

## Evaluation

Of the eighteen regular packages in the secondary school reading portion of the sequence, ten require the student to prove his mastery of the learning package by passing an objective test. To provide for these tests, a testing center is open approximately twenty-five hours per week, during which time a student may take any of the objective tests available in reading or in any other portion of the sequence. Tests are scored by computer, and an IBM printout is posted to show the results. Other evaluations in reading include analyzing and evaluating a secondary reading test, finding the readability of certain secondary material, locating high-interest books, and making a lesson plan which incorporates assignment readiness, SQ3R skills, and reading study skills. These latter evaluations are scored by the team reading specialist who then gives feedback directly to the student.

## Conclusion

The reading preparation program at Illinois State University represents a fundamental shift in the instructional focus for preparation of secondary level preservice teachers. Essentially, this competency based program offers the preservice teacher the opportunity to acquire the knowledge and skills relative to working with secondary school reading problems within a framework that is self-paced and largely self-directive. While the program is still relatively new, its theoretical base has had considerable impact on the development of new instructional approaches in both the public school and the university domain. Such a transition from a course-centered structure has not been without its problems. This new program requires constant attention and revision with respect to the scope of instructional objectives, desirable learning activities, alternative sensory approaches, and ways of facilitating equitable evaluations.

**Reference**

1. Kibler, Robert J. *Behavioral Objectives and Instruction.* Boston: Allyn and Bacon, 1970, 18-20.

# COMPETENCIES FOR TEACHERS OF READING AND OTHER LANGUAGE ARTS

*Harry W. Sartain*
*University of Pittsburgh*

Specific teacher competencies are the instructional objectives of any teacher-education program. But we teacher educators, like all other educators, seem to have the same enthusiasm for stating and studying instructional objectives as we have for going to the dentist. Slighting objectives, however, like slighting dental visits, can be a foolish practice that results in greatly reduced effectiveness. When objectives are vague, instructional time is used inefficiently, learning effort is dissipated, and students grow into inadequate teachers.

The writing of teacher competencies and other educational objectives is especially difficult because authorities hold such strongly divergent opinions on the matter. It is therefore necessary to seek agreement upon a list of criteria which will be followed in itemizing competencies. Only after reaching agreement on the criteria can there be any hope of reaching agreement on the competencies.

A proposed list of criteria for the stating of competencies for teachers of reading and the related language arts follows *(4)*.

1. Competency statements should reflect a recognition of the basic interrelationships among the language arts.

Oral language skills are the foundation for reading skills, and an understanding of the structure and mechanics of written language is also required for fluent reading. Therefore, no teacher can be a fully effective reading instructor without having the competencies needed for teaching or for cooperating with others in teaching the child the related language understandings, attitudes, and skills.

2. Competency statements should be worded in a simple, straightforward manner so that they can be easily understood and utilized by the learner and the instructor.

Competencies and other objectives which appear to have been written to impress the reader with the writer's erudition or his skill in using a thesaurus usually have had no appreciable effect upon educational practice.

3. Competency statements should be specific and detailed enough to provide clear guidance for students and instructors but also be brief enough to be assimilated and used.

In the past, some statements have been so broad as to be mere platitudes. Others have been so detailed, repetitive, and voluminous that they have overwhelmed the student and the instructor with verbiage, thereby providing no help in planning teacher-education experiences which can be completed within reasonable time limits.

4. Competency statements should specify or clearly imply desired teaching-learning acts or behaviors.

There has been a great deal of disagreement concerning the adequacy of goals stated as behavioral outcomes. The humanist suspects the behavioral psychologist of attempting to mold children's minds in a predetermined "brave new world" style that would minimize individuality. Beck responds to this criticism by showing that some humanist teachers set goals that are too vague to be helpful, and she adds that "we cannot afford to ignore what the behaviorists have learned if we are to teach effectively the goals that humanists hold" (1).

Educators have been critical, also, when behaviorists have declared that no educational objective should be stated if the instructional outcome cannot be measured. Since this too often is interpreted as "if the instructional outcome cannot be *easily* measured by traditional instruments," it would mean the elimination of all objectives leading to the development of attitudes, appreciations, and values. Obviously, these are among the most important objectives of instruction in literature, as well as in civilized human relations, and their elimination is unthinkable to any but the simpleminded. Instead, we must specify the objectives that we deem important and then seek new ways of observing and measuring behaviors that indicate progress toward their achievement.

5. In relation to each general competency there *may* be specific statements that imply several kinds of behaviors:

    Valuing—displaying positive attitudes toward the children, the profession, and the communication arts

    Understanding—knowing the concepts and principles to be taught

Applying—using knowledge of how to teach in working with learners

Analyzing-Changing—evaluating professional processes and devising new and better teaching techniques

While taxonomies by Bloom (2) and by Krothwahl (3) are extremely helpful in stimulating thinking about educational objectives, if one follows them slavishly, the result is wordy and repetitious. In actual practice the observation of one behavior can imply the fulfillment of more than one closely related goal, making it unnecessary to itemize every degree of development.

6.  The behaviors which are specified as examples of expected outcomes should include a variety of options in order to foster the development of human individuality.

An error frequently made in connection with the preparation of behavioral objectives has been that of stating only one behavior as the criterion for the attainment of each understanding, skill, or attitude. For example, when intending to teach children to understand and enjoy a literary characterization by identifying with the character in a story, the teacher might state the objective as: "Describes the enthusiasm he would feel if he were in the position of Teddy Roosevelt in Frances Cavanah's story 'A Naturalist in the City.' " But any child who is repelled by the thought of white mice or a fresh seal's skin might react quite differently from what the teacher intended even though that child were very able to identify fully with characters in other stories.

Likewise, in the preparation of teachers of reading one might state a competency such as this: "Adapts reading instruction suitably for children having subtle learning disabilities by providing Frostig exercises." Then, if the standard were applied consistently, the behavior of a student teacher would be assessed negatively if she were following a fine, cooperating teacher's example by using the Fernald techniques and other procedures that have been proven productive.

In both of these instances, the learner would not be given credit for achieving the outcome because the criterion behavior was too limited to allow other valid performances. This point clearly illustrates the importance of permitting optional behaviors as evidence of learning.

7.  Competencies should be stated at the entry level, the advanced level, and the specialization level, when appropriate, to indicate growth in capability.

It is impossible for a beginning teacher to have mastered all of the skills of reading instruction. Competency statements, therefore, should indicate which capabilities are essential at the beginning of teaching and which are to be developed through additional study and inservice work.

8. Competency statements may be grouped in such a way that they are an aid to teacher educators in planning blocks or modules of experiences which can be built into teacher-education programs and inservice programs.

The preparation of an excellent teacher of reading is a long process. Consequently, the program of preparation must be divided into meaningful segments. These segments may be developed around different groups of competencies and around the stages of advancement toward specialization.

## Competency Statements in Modules of Teacher Education

In written form a module might consist of only a list of the competencies pertaining to a particular phase of teaching. Or it might also include appropriate learning experiences and the criterion behaviors that indicate satisfactory attainment of the competencies.

Some modules, such as the following, should be fundamental to the preparation of all teachers:

- Understanding Self
- Understanding the Child
- Understanding How the Child Learns
- Understanding and Working in the Community

Other modules should focus upon the learnings that pertain directly to the teaching of reading (4):

- Understanding the Communications Processes and the Structure of the English Language
- Interaction with Parents and the Community
- Instructional Planning: Curriculum, Instructional Steps, Materials, Approaches
- Evaluation and Diagnosis of Learning
- School and Classroom Organization for Individualizing Instruction
- Individualizing Instruction in Difficult Circumstances (economically underprivileged, bilingual, nonstandard dialects)
- Developing Language Fluency and Perceptual Skills in Childhood
- Reception and Expression of Social Communications
- Teaching Vocabulary and Word Attack Skills

- Teaching the Decoding and Retention of Factual Information (comprehension)
- Teaching Functional Reading and Study Skills in Specific Fields of Content
- Teaching Literary Appreciation for Young Children
- Teaching Literary Appreciation for Intermediate Children
- Teaching Literary Appreciation for Secondary and College Students
- Corrective Treatment of Reading Difficulties in the Classroom
- Clinical Treatment of Reading Difficulties
- Initiating Improvements in School Programs

The listing of competencies of varied types and levels of advancement and the development of modules for teacher education are extremely demanding undertakings. However, the usefulness of these modules when fitted into preservice and inservice programs should be tremendous. Because they will precisely itemize productive instructional behaviors, the modules should help us all in the task to which we are dedicated—the preparation of excellent teachers of reading.

### References

1.  Beck, Isabel. "Toward Humanistic Goals Through Behavioral Objectives," in John Maxwell and Anthony Tovatt (Eds.), *On Writing Behavioral Objectives for English.* Champaign, Illinois: National Council of Teachers of English, 1970, 97-105.

2.  Bloom, Benjamin S., et al. (Eds.). *Taxonomy of Educational Objectives: Handbook I, Cognitive Domain.* New York: David McKay, 1956.

3.  Krathwohl, David R., et al. (Eds.). *Taxonomy of Educational Objectives: Handbook II, Affective Domain.* New York: David McKay, 1964.

4.  Sartain, Harry W., and Paul E. Stanton (Eds.). *Modular Preparation for Teaching Reading.* Newark, Delaware: International Reading Association, 1974.

# THE TOTALITY APPROACH
# IN TEACHING READING

*J. Allen Figurel*
*Indiana University Northwest*

To meet the national challenges of The Right to Read, schools need to focus on change since the past methods have not produced effective reading for all. Students are individuals with individual characteristics in everything, including the best method of learning to read; teachers are different with different personalities and preferentials in the way they teach reading. Schools need more flexibility in determining curricula, methods, curriculum materials, and instructional aids. The degree of variation in reading instruction will determine how teachers and pupils interact to produce efficient readers at every level of educational development. There are both individual and group developmental tasks that need to be taken into account in the education of American children. All individual instruction will not develop a child to interact in a group situation, nor will all group instruction further learning to read since many children have their own individual learning patterns. A combination, therefore, based on individual as well as group learning requirements is to be made if The Right to Read is to be achieved for all children.

The most important function of the elementary school is to teach language and mathematics skills; all else will be added if this portion is done since a child skilled in reading, writing, spelling, and mathematics can make the grade at whatever task he may choose. This paper is concerned with the development of reading abilities in all children; therefore, the rest of the discussion is pinpointed to it. With the totality approach described herein, more educable children will be able to read at grade levels or above.

The rationale for bringing about successful reading achievement for all children is based on the assumption that the practice teaching director of a university reading department works with a city school corporation—its administrators, supervisors, principals, and supervising teachers with their paraprofessionals—to form a team which will train future teachers to teach with a totality approach. The team will also train supervising teachers and others to utilize all the resources of the university and the school organization to train student teachers to diagnose and discover the best way for achieving a high reading potential for each child and also to train the supervising teachers to see the advantages of the total approach and to put it into practice not only in the basic reading period but throughout the school day in all activities. The use of paraprofessionals, the room mother, and children themselves in the total reading act makes everyone a teacher and a learner. The coordinator of such a program is the reading instructor of the university assisted by the director of the reading clinic or laboratory.

The activities for the total teaching act begin in the reading clinic of a university which is well equipped with all sorts of reading materials: reading aids in the form of games, individual working exercises, wheel phonograms, the Language Master, the Controlled Reader, the Hoffman Reader, SRA reading boxes, perception training materials, projectors, slides, talking books, visual training materials, pacers, guiders, tachistoscopes, cassettes, and other tape recorders; a variety of tables and carrels along the walls equipped with headsets, listening programs, school newspapers, study skills programs, workbooks, a TV receiver; a variety of hardware such as overhead projectors, transparency making machines, a primary typewriter, several other typewriters, record players, instructional tapes, CAI machines, and videorecorders; and a host of other small items that teachers may find useful in diagnosing and training readers. Some hardware is desirable but not essential. If funds are available, a number of satellite centers may be located in some schools throughout the university's sphere of influence. The satellite centers may contain some of the same teaching materials and devices and may be connected electrically with the home center at the university. Satellite centers serving disadvantaged areas will have an oversupply of speech reproducing and speech recording machines for use with such children who have dialect problems or speak a foreign language. If there are children who speak only a foreign language, materials containing the foreign language and English should be coordinated.

The remainder of this paper explains how materials are used, where they are used, and what part the various personnel of instruction play in such an organization. Based on the particular needs of each student, the program is not planned for a year but is organized developmentally.

## The Beginning of the Instruction
## and Teacher Training Program

After the student has completed a course in teaching reading and is ready for student teaching, she is assigned to one of the reading clinics for a period of time depending on how quickly she is able to diagnose the reading disabilities of one youngster and plan a program of instruction for him including such things as behavioral objectives in the cognitive domain, the affective domain, and perhaps the psychomotor domain, if needed. Her next step will be a one-to-one teaching of her particular child as she learns to know him as an individual and also his learning preferentials. The instructional activity is supervised by the clinic supervisor who knows the reading instructional program as taught by the university instructor. This experience teaches the student teacher the importance of knowing each child individually, what he is like, and how he learns best to read.

The student teacher's second step is to do microteaching with five or six pupils selected from the room of her supervising teacher. Again, careful planning is done before and during the actual teaching. The microteaching may be done in some section of her school or room; or, if necessary, she may take the pupils to one of the small rooms of the reading clinic. The plan, as stated before, includes determining the behavioral objectives that are needed for this particular group of youngsters and evaluating the results based on the objectives selected. Some videotaping is done for this microteaching experience. The videotapes are then discussed with the student. In the discussion period the supervising teacher is always included, and at times, the university instructor also. Strengths are pointed out first and then the ways in which the lessons could be improved. Other teachers may be invited for the showing of the tapes, and often the tapes of several students are shown at one sitting. This procedure has the effect of improving not only the teaching of the student teachers but also that of the supervising teacher and other teachers in the building. These showings are directed by the university instructor. He, too, may learn that some changes can improve his class instruction.

## Macroteaching as the Total Teaching Act

Macroteaching is the final training period for the student teacher. In this step of her preparation she assumes control of the entire room, helps the supervising teacher in the organization, and along with the latter plans the necessary instructional steps for effective reading instruction. She and the supervising teacher plan the behavioral objectives desired for the different groups in the room. She usually observes at first the particular pattern of teaching used by the supervising teacher. A conference follows each observation. The university instructor may be included in the conference period, and at times even in the teaching period. Gradually the student teacher assumes the teaching of a group. She is made responsible for planning and selecting materials of instruction and audiovisuals, if necessary. Her plan for the lesson is usually done beforehand and is approved by the supervising teacher and, if necessary, by the college instructor.

## The Neglected Element

Throughout the land elementary teachers have a schedule which they follow meticulously. They assign twenty minutes of reading, for instance, for Group I (the fast group), twenty minutes for Group II (the middle group), and twenty minutes for Group III (the slow group); therefore each group gets the same amount of time for reading. As each group finishes its reading period with the teacher, the children of the group go to their seats to do seatwork, dittoed sheets or workbooks, prepared either by the teacher or the para-professional. Often the seatwork does not correlate with the lesson just finished and, thus, becomes busywork.

The time element is invariably ignored by most teachers as it applies to different groups. Rarely does the teacher attune the time to the needs of the group. Everyone knows that the fast group covers more pages in the readers and the slow group merely manages to cover a minimal number of pages. The middle group is happy for it covers exactly the reading materials assigned for the grade. By what reasoning can it be assumed that each group needs the same block of reading time? Isn't it wise to realize that the slow group may need twice as much time to complete a lesson which the fast group completes in half of the allowed time? Would it not be more sensible to allot reading time on the basis of the needs of the children? It may be necessary to have two or even three reading periods for the slow learners so that they may keep up with their grade level. Behavioral objectives for a group may resemble those of other groups, but the time needed to learn such behavioral objectives may have to be double or triple that of the fast group.

The *terrible* IQ may be the cause of student failure in reading. The expectations in learning for such children are often very low in the minds of many teachers. Teachers often forget that they get just what they expect from children. And the *obnoxious* IQ fixes in the teacher's mind when to expect much and when to expect very little. Teachers most often get just what they expect from children. Year after year the slow children get further behind in grade levels and finally drop out of school as soon as the law permits. They are not prepared for jobs, and as a result they become dropouts without work, join street gangs, and become terrors to the community. At this level they reach the high point of *progressive retardation*.

Some school districts have suspended giving small children IQ tests. Educators have found that teachers do not prejudge a child's reading success so quickly when they do not have a prefixed notion of a child's reading potential; instead they keep on expecting much more from all the children and, consequently, are more successful in teaching reading. In ghetto areas, contracted schools usually follow an individual pattern of learning, and teachers and teacher aides encourage children right along. A child does not lose his self-esteem, for he is not competing with others but with himself. And the time needed to learn certain behavioral objectives in reading is not prescribed. Children spend as much time as is necessary for learning a task before they move to the next one. The trend now is toward individualized instruction. If teachers regulate the time element in their teaching, they will soon discover that at the end of the school term all children will be reading at grade level or better. This is what commercial firms are selling to our administrators—a year's progress for each year in school excluding, of course, those students that have had long periods of absence.

## How About the Content Field?

Content in the elementary school is minimal. As was said at the beginning of this paper, the main function of the elementary school is to teach language and mathematics skills. If this goal is accomplished, all else will be added later. The writer has heard teachers say, "How am I going to get my art and music in—and history and science, too—if I spend so much time on reading?" And the writer's answer is simple: "What good is art, music, science, or history if, when the child gets into high school, he can't read?" If he can read, he will learn more art, music, science, and history in several months in junior high school.

The writer does not advocate dropping music, art, science, and history in the elementary school. They have their place in the curriculum but only as aids to learning to read through the use of these subjects. The student teachers, the supervising teachers, and other teachers have an obligation to begin to teach children how to read social studies materials, science materials, and newspapers. The directed reading lesson plan for the content subjects does not differ materially from that of the reading lesson. First, there is the teacher's motivation followed by presentation of the new and unknown words found in the content lesson. This work is followed by guided silent reading (done at home if so desired) in which the teacher sets the purpose for the reading: What am I to look for in this lesson? For example, what did John do to earn money to buy a pet? The purpose for the content lesson should be very specific so that children know specifically what they are looking for when they read the history or the science lesson. The follow up of such lessons will, of course, use discussions and other activities.

Student teachers should be trained to teach the content subjects through reading. They may be teaching one group while the supervising teacher is teaching another. Again, teaching the content subjects effectively may have to involve the methods teacher at the university. Inservice programs may include lessons in these areas either through actual observation or through the use of videotaping. Music and art should be outcomes of lessons in the various subjects, including reading. Paraprofessionals become aides in any school activity. If the aide is a mother of one of the children in school, she can assist the regular teacher and the practice teacher in planning the use of community resources available in the district. This procedure results in better public relations and a sympathetic view of the school by all people living in the district.

During the instructional periods in the school, teachers, student teachers, and others may find individual drawbacks which prohibit some children from successfully learning. These children should be referred to the clinic. The supervising teacher may be the coordinator of a remedial program and serve as liaison between the school and the clinic. A good clinic can discover the cause of the retardation and assign one of the clinic workers to do the remediation or send the suggested plan for remediation back to the school for implementation. It must be remembered that satellite centers can be used for diagnosis; and in the casework, they have the resource of the central university clinic.

## Conclusion

The recommendations and implementations discussed in this paper should produce children who are reading at their proper levels. An elaborate clinic is not essential if the teachers have been trained in diagnosing reading problems and planning for their remediation. The contracted schools make exactly the same promise: to have every child reading at grade level. In order to maintain the dignity of the teaching profession, parents and administrators must be shown that schools can do a professional job of educating all young Americans regardless of race, religion, or national origin. American educators have no other course of action.

# A NATIONAL SURVEY
# OF METHODS COURSES

*Harold H. Roeder*
*State University of New York*
*College at Fredonia*

During the past decade, research studies have revealed that the teacher is one of the most important variables in reading instruction (*1,3,4*). Unfortunately, very few researchers have attempted to establish whether colleges and universities are preparing teachers to carry out this task.

When a teacher is graduated from an accredited institution and awarded some form of state certification, it is often assumed that he possesses at least a minimal understanding of how to teach reading. However, due to the variations which exist in institutional and state certification requirements, there is no guarantee that the graduates of all elementary education sequences have completed a course in reading methods. As a matter of fact, one researcher involved in this investigation received his baccalaureate degree in elementary education from an institution which required such courses as industrial arts (three hours), music methods (six hours), arts and crafts for classroom teachers (six hours), physical education (two hours), and marriage and family relations (three hours). When this graduate embarked upon his professional career, he was prepared consequently, to teach his fifth graders how to swim, sing, make puppets, build bird houses, play volleyball, settle family arguments, and weave baskets. Unfortunately, he was not prepared to teach his students how to analyze words, comprehend printed materials, or critically evaluate textbook selections. Somehow, his old alma mater had let him down; it had disregarded the most important R—reading. Although he had fulfilled all of the requirements for graduation and state certification, he and his contemporaries were never required to complete a course in the teaching of reading.

Instruction in reading methods was relegated to a two-week segment of a language arts course. It was sandwiched in among creative writing, poetry, choral speaking, how to teach spelling, developing listening skills, teaching correct grammar, and letter writing. If a prospective teacher happened to be absent from the language arts sessions which dealt with the teaching of reading, he never met Dick and Jane, Jack and Janet, Tip and Mitten, or anyone else in the area of reading.

Succinctly stated, the purpose of this investigation was to ascertain how many colleges and universities throughout the United States require prospective elementary teachers to complete a course in the teaching of reading.

## Procedures

*Criteria.* The colleges and universities which were included in this investigation met the following criteria:

1. Each institution offered an undergraduate elementary education sequence.
2. The undergraduate elementary education sequence was considered to be a major institutional offering.
3. Each institution was a four-year college or university.
4. In states where appropriate, each elementary education sequence was approved by the state education department.
5. The elementary education curriculum of each institution was regionally accredited by the appropriate regional accrediting commission.
6. The elementary education curriculum of each institution had functioned for a minimum of four years.

*Population.* Identification of the population which met the criteria established for this investigation was not an easy task. Reference sources (2,6,7) reported that in 1970 there were over twelve hundred approved teacher-education programs in the United States. This totally encompassing figure included: four-year colleges and universities, junior colleges, graduate offerings, undergraduate offerings, and all types of curricula from highly specialized areas of study, such as art and music, to miscellaneous elementary education sequences. Identification of the population was also impeded by erroneous and incomplete listings which appeared in the sources.

A total of 940 colleges and universities appeared to meet the criteria. All states and the District of Columbia were represented in this population.

*Data collection.* A questionnaire which requested data on several aspects of teacher preparation was mailed to the president of each institution. In most instances, the questionnaire was forwarded to the administrator who was directly responsible for the elementary education curriculum. Two follow-up inquiries were mailed to non-respondents. A total of 97.3 percent (N=915) of the colleges and universities contacted responded. In 32 of the states, returns of 100 percent were recorded.

The willingness of respondents to return completed question-naires was attributed to two factors. First, the questionnaire was as concise and unambiguous as possible; pretests eliminated any difficulties which had appeared to exist. Second, the correspondence which accompanied each questionnaire assumed the appearance of a personal request for information by printing the letters without the inside address, salutation, and signature. Later, matching type was used to insert the appropriate inside address and salutation. Finally, each letter was personally signed by one of the researchers.

Of the 915 responses which were received, 860 were usable, 9 provided insufficient data, 44 institutions reported that they did not offer undergraduate elementary education sequences, and 2 responses were received after the data were analyzed.

*Analysis of the data.* Approximately 18 percent (N=156) of the institutions which were surveyed did not report course work in semester hours; consequently, a conversion table was devised. It was based on a 3:2 ratio (quarter hours to semester hours) similar to the type of procedure which registrars use in establishing credit for transfer students. Other variations in reporting were resolved through the use of appropriate coding procedures.

## Major Findings

It was gratifying to discover that the majority of colleges and universities which were surveyed required prospective elementary teachers to complete a course in the teaching of reading. As indicated in Table 1, most institutions also required prospective teachers to complete courses in language arts and children's literature.

*Reading.* Approximately 89 percent (88.6 percent/N=763) of the institutions which were surveyed required a course in the teaching of reading. Of the 143 (16.6 percent) institutions which combined the teaching of reading with another methods course, 110 institutions incorporated instruction in reading methods and language arts. It was interesting to note that only 42 of the institutions which combined these two courses allocated more than three semester hours of credit to the combined course.

Although it is not revealed in Table 1, approximately 3 percent (N=26) of the institutions which were surveyed offered highly specialized courses in reading, such as Reading for Urban Teachers and Diagnosis for Classroom Teachers.

## Related Findings

*Language arts.* Over 83 percent (83.2 percent/N=715) of the institutions which were surveyed required a course in language arts. As Table 1 indicates 256 (29.8 percent) of the institutions combined instruction in language arts with preparation in at least one other content area.

*Children's literature.* Although an understanding and appreciation of children's literature are essential to the teacher of reading, 19.4 percent (N=167) of the institutions did not require such a course.

*Evaluation.* Approximately 58 percent (57.7 percent/N=496) of the institutions surveyed did not require prospective teachers to complete a course in "tests and measures." Only 7.2 percent (N=62) of the institutions reported that this area of instruction was a major component of another course. These data raise an interesting question: If elementary teachers are expected to select, administer, score, interpret, and implement the findings of standardized and informal reading instruments, when and where is the necessary preparation obtained?

**TABLE 1**
Nationwide Summary of Specific Methods
Requirements for Classroom Teachers

| Courses | No Hours | | 1 - 2 Hrs. | | 3 Hrs. | | 4 - 5 Hrs. | |
|---|---|---|---|---|---|---|---|---|
| | Freq. | Pct. | Freq. | Pct. | Freq. | Pct. | Freq. | Pct. |
| Reading Methods | 86 | 10.0 | 118 | 13.7 | 408 | 47.4 | 68 | 7.9 |
| Language Arts | 102 | 11.8 | 181 | 21.1 | 237 | 27.6 | 27 | 3.1 |
| Children's Lit. | 167 | 19.4 | 162 | 18.8 | 397 | 46.2 | 23 | 2.7 |
| Evaluation | 496 | 57.7 | 104 | 12.1 | 153 | 17.8 | 10 | 1.2 |

| Courses | 6+ Hrs. | | Combined | | Unscorable* | | TOTAL | |
|---|---|---|---|---|---|---|---|---|
| | Freq. | Pct. | Freq. | Pct. | Freq. | Pct. | Freq. | Pct. |
| Reading Methods | 26 | 3.0 | 143 | 16.6 | 11 | 1.4 | 860 | 100.0 |
| Language Arts | 14 | 1.6 | 256 | 19.8 | 43 | 5.0 | 860 | 100.0 |
| Children's Lit. | 4 | .5 | 63 | 7.3 | 44 | 5.2 | 860 | 100.0 |
| Evaluation | 2 | .2 | 62 | 7.2 | 33 | 3.8 | 860 | 100.0 |

*Restricted choice or confused response

## Limitations of the Research

In addition to the difficulties which were encountered in identifying the institutions which met the established criteria, two other limitations were noted. First, this investigation disregarded the preparation of those individuals who did not complete an elementary education sequence but who eventually became classroom teachers. Second, it was impossible to evaluate adequately the quality and content of the required reading methods courses.

## Concluding Statement

Requiring a course in the teaching of reading is certainly not a panacea. Prospective teachers may sit through two, four, or six hours of instruction and remain virtually unchanged. Naturally, a great deal depends upon the quality of instruction and the commitment of the student. Requiring a course in reading methods or a related reading course, however, does have certain advantages. It emphasizes the importance of reading as an area of instruction, commits institutional and state funds for the financial support of the course or courses, and guarantees the appointment of faculty members to teach the courses.

Although the colleges and universities which were surveyed left little doubt that they were attempting to prepare elementary teachers to teach reading, perhaps they have not gone far enough. Ten percent of the institutions which were surveyed did not require students to complete a course in reading methods. Also, most of the 143 institutions which incorporated the teaching of reading with instruction in at least one other methods course did not allocate the amount of time and course credit which the combined course merited. Finally, while only 94 institutions required prospective teachers to complete more than three semester hours of course work in the teaching of reading, 133 institutions required more than three semester hours in art methods for classroom teachers; 152 institutions, more than three semester hours in music methods; 298 institutions, more than three hours in physical education; 252 institutions, more than three semester hours in religion and theology; and 124 institutions, more than three semester hours in geography.

It is difficult to comprehend why prospective elementary teachers should be required to complete an excessive number of hours in such subjects. Perhaps, though, requiring four or more hours in "religion" can be justified: if a beginning teacher is expected to teach reading and has not been adequately prepared for the task, he had better know how to pray.

## References

1. Bond, Guy L., and Robert Dykstra. *Coordinating Center for First Grade Reading Instruction Programs.* Minneapolis: University of Minnesota, 1967.

2. Federation of Regional Accrediting Commission of Higher Education. *Accredited Institutions of Higher Education 1969-1970.* Washington, D. C.: American Council of Higher Education, 1969.

3. Eller, William. "Contributions of the First and Second Grade Studies," in J. Allen Figurel (Ed.), *Reading and Realism,* 1968 Proceedings, Volume 13, Part 1. Newark, Delaware: International Reading Association, 1969.

4. Fry, Edward B. "First Grade Reading Instruction Using Diacritical Marking System, Initial Teaching Alphabet, and Basal Reader System," *Reading Teacher,* 19 (May 1966), 666-669.

5. Mayor, John R. *Accreditation in Teacher Education: Its Influence on Higher Education.* Washington, D. C.: National Commission on Accrediting, 1965.

6. Singletary, Otis (Ed.). *American Universities and Colleges* (10th ed.). Washington, D. C.: American Council on Education, 1968.

7. Stinnett, Timothy M. *A Manual on Certification Requirements for School Personnel in the United States 1970 Edition.* Washington, D. C.: National Education Association, 1970.

8. Woellner, Elizabeth H., and M. Aurilla Wood. *Requirements for Certification 1969-1970.* Chicago: University of Chicago Press, 1969.

# COGNITIVE ORGANIZERS
# FOR PRESERVICE TEACHER EDUCATION

*Joseph Ilika*
*Texas A & M University*

The singular content issue facing methods of reading instructors in the 1960s concerned the information explosion (*25*) and the materials explosion (*30*). If thirty students self-select 20 different journal articles from the past forty years, the duplication of readings within 600 articles read is rarely over 10 articles! Reading about reading poses a problem of developing some structure to organize the ideas acquired. Clearly, a plea for the identification of valid structures in reading pedagogy is in order.

## A Philosophy of Content

As reading knowledge and materials increase at a geometric rate (*25*), teachers need to be preorganized to code and to categorize reading knowledge for instructional improvement. To accomplish this feat, Bruner's concept of knowledge structure may be used as a stepping stone to cognitive organization and economy. Thus, as Bruner (*11*) states:

> Knowledge is a model we construct to give meaning and structure to regularities in experience. The organizing ideas of any body of knowledge are inventions for rendering experience economical and connected. We invent concepts such as force in physics, the bond in chemistry, motives in psychology, style in literature as means to the end of comprehension. . . . The power of great organizing concepts is in large part that they permit us to understand and sometimes to predict or change the world in which we live. But their power lies also in the fact that ideas provide instruments for experience.

Clearly, the implication is that course content needs to be relevant to the regularities of reading experience. No matter how distasteful the avant-garde in the professional reading community may regard the singular finding of Barton and Wilder (6) and Austin and Morrison (2), the facts are that basal reading programs (BRP) are the main methods of reading instruction and that BRPs will be here for some time to come. It can be argued that BRPs must be the most meaningful among the rank and file teacher practitioners, pending research to show otherwise (27). Basal readers, therefore, need to be recognized as a basis for the development of a structure of reading knowledge. The position taken here is that BRPs may be exploited as cognitive organizers for the purpose of creating a structure for reading knowledge as a basis for a productive cognitive economy for teachers. A cognitive economy suggests that teachers need structure for the categorization of reading knowledge input for immediate or ultimate output on behalf of improved instruction. The structure ought to be simple, functional, and meaningful to the majority of teachers. A rationale for the development of reading content structure around BRP is as follows:

1. Research shows that basal readers dominate the means to reading instruction.
2. Basal reading concepts have more meaning for the majority of reading teachers than do any other systems.
3. Other existing methods, such as language experience and individualized reading, are still relatively rare and may require more expertise than what can be accomplished through a typical reading methods course (27).
4. On the whole, new teachers are expected to conform to local basal reading practices. Teachers totally unfamiliar with BRP strategy are vulnerable to unnecessary anxiety and insecurity at a crucial professional period.
5. Preservice course content should thoroughly orient teachers to the reading skills and/or reading behavioral objectives subsumed in teachers' manuals.
6. Preservice course content should seek to improve reading instruction "within the system" (e.g., suggest workable alternatives to traditional barbershop reading).
7. The mastery of skills and knowledge subsumed under basal reading systems are prerequisites to understanding the rationale, as well as the utilization of more complex systems such as language experience, individualized reading, and programed reading.
8. The structure of reading course content should provide for the addition of new knowledge, methods, and materials, which purport to accomplish more efficiently the core reading behavioral objectives of basal readers.

9. The learning of course content should constantly reinforce a structure of reading knowledge and demonstrate how new ideas are related to existing structures at their most commonly understood level.

10. Emphasis on BRP strategy does not neglect the content and skills necessary to other systems of reading instruction; on the contrary, other systems are analyzed for possibilities in counteracting BRP weaknesses.

11. Mastery and skill in BRP when coupled with the structure of reading knowledge are means to the development of an adaptive teacher who may categorize and evaluate new reading knowledge and methods for the improvement of reading instruction.

The preceding rationale ought to contribute to the prevention of a state of information overload (25) and aid in the creation of a teacher who may cope with staggering inputs of new reading content, new materials, and other innovations. A few notions of how content purposes may be attained are described in the remaining portion of the paper.

## The Overlapping Structure of Basal Readers

Stauffer (33) states:

> Emmett Betts was quite right when he said that in general authors of basal readers were in agreement on the basic principles and assumptions regarding directed reading activities.

A systematic comparison of old and new basal reading lesson plans needs to be identified, therefore, for overlapping structure, somewhat as Betts (7) reports. Thus, the continuity of the old and the emergence of new developments as expounded by Stauffer (33) in his Directed Reading Thinking Activity may be understood. From a critical analysis of BRP lesson plans, the strengths and weaknesses of basals can be identified also (31).

The writer finds that one way to develop student awareness of structure is to assign students the task of comparing the topic headings of lesson plans and stories of two different basal reading publishers. Subsequently, students share their findings to rediscover the overlapping structures as Betts and Stauffer have previously noted.

From the preceding analysis of reading lesson plans, the students can rapidly master the concepts of readiness, motivating questions, ongoing questions (mathemagenic behavior questions), silent and purposeful oral reading, comprehension and word analysis skill development, and supplementary reading activity variations. It is the instructor's duty to review and relate "previously learned learning theory" to the outcome of lesson plan analysis.

The most glaring weakness of a student in writing lesson plans with basal models is the inability to include activities to develop comprehension and word analysis skills and plans for individualization. These areas of weaknesses can be brought into clearer focus by teacher interviews and critical reviews of materials and various reading strategies.

## Teacher Interviews as a Means of Developing Reading Content Structure

Keeping in mind Guzsak's implied message of relevance and irrelevance in content (*28*), the teacher interview is assigned to enlighten the neophyte students with reading instructional reality. The following preorganizers for the interview and for related course content are given to the student:

### Sample Interview Assignment

*Purpose.* Since most of you have not had close contact with classroom situations and reading instruction, I feel it is necessary to have you interview actively involved reading teachers. From such an experience you should derive insight into some of the following factors related to an elementary school reading program.

1. Type of program: basal, individualized, programed.
2. Number of children in the class.
3. Range of individual differences.
4. Availability of library books and other materials.
5. Classroom floor plans and reading group organizations.

You should feel free to discuss these matters in interview. By all means arrange to interview friends or acquaintances in order to speed up rapport and help you to get more insight into a "live reading program." Please have at least one interview completed for class feedback.

Discovery of essences of structure through interviews and subsequent feedback to the class reveal an inevitable variety of insights. Interview experience data form a quick referential basis for course text content objectives. Students are amazed at the variation of basal reading organization patterns and the variation in the availability of materials. Their discoveries of teacher teaching styles are related to Betts' hierarchy of teacher competency (*7*).

Interview data also elicit an awareness of the importance of the teacher's knowledge of word analysis skills and reading resource material.

## Developing Teacher Knowledge of
## Word Analysis Skills

A strategy to help the undergraduate become aware of her need for word analysis knowledge is to pretest students with Henriksen's Teacher Word Analysis Test (HTWAT) and to familiarize students with research by Shannon (29), Farinella (19), Gagon (20), and Henriksen (21).

The HTWAT is administered early in the semester. An overnight computer scored feedback of total subtest scores and total scores is given to the students from a computer printout. Each student is urged to identify his low subtest areas and to compare his mean scores with previous class scores. Emphasis is placed on self-study in a programed test for word analysis knowledge, such as Wilson and Hall (35). The unit on word analysis skills is enriched by research finding handouts from Clymer (14), Bailey (55), Burmeister (12), and Aaron (1).

The HTWAT is readministered at the end of the course, and students are given immediate feedback. Results usually indicate growth. Students are urged to extend studies in weak word analysis areas. However, since Shannon (29) and Cordts (15, 16) find teachers and undergraduates deficient in auditory discrimination, a further probe of this area has been conducted with the California Phonics Survey (CPS). On the basis of the CPS scores, students who have scored 65 or below are asked to read, listen, and respond to Brown's (9) *Letters, Sounds, and Words* (LSW) programed phonics, and to seventeen tapes which are correlated to LSW. Results reveal that the students who score low on the CPS benefit from the program and tapes and make significant improvement on Form II of the CPS. The astonishing reaction to this branching course content for approximately 10 percent of the students is that the students who score high on the CPS eagerly wish to participate in the programs.

The word analysis unit is also used as a model to demonstrate how provisions for diagnosing individual differences can be followed up at the college level with a five-station listening laboratory operated on a self-directed and self-help basis. These efforts to increase word analysis knowledge and skills are constantly related to the core of word analysis content of the reading lesson plan structure of the basal reader and, thus, attempt to build structure, as mentioned earlier. Students are also reminded that their mastery of word analysis skills must be exceedingly high if they wish to be competent and secure in the more sophisticated levels of reading instruction involving language experience and individualized reading as described by Betts (7).

As a result of this word analysis unit, there is evidence (22) to indicate that, contrary to the earlier findings of Shannon (29) and the more recent ones by Henriksen (21), methods of reading courses can indeed increase the word analysis knowledge of teachers. Student interview data also reveal that mature and versatile teachers utilize a variety of materials to improve the reading skills of children reading on multilevels.

## Relating Reading Materials to the Basal Reading Programs

Teacher interviews, observation of new materials at book exhibits, and curriculum laboratories reveal that students are amazed at the variety of non-BRP materials and programs. As a rule, students are eager to examine new materials.

The cognitive organizer, "Reading Resource Preview Guide," forms a strategy for discovering new reading resource and method structures and for sharing findings with members of the class.

### Sample Reading Resource Preview Guide

*Task.* Select a set of materials for intense study and share it with the class.

*Purposes*

1. To acquaint teachers with reading resources and various methods.
2. To consider the applicability of new resources to pupil reading needs.
3. To develop teacher awareness of the structure and/or the strategies of reading labs, kits, special series of texts, programs, and treatises on methods.
4. To give teachers insight into methods of motivating reading, teaching reading skills, diagnosing reading needs, assigning reading tasks, administering informal tests, seeing the relationships among basal reader lesson plans, and evaluating reading growth in terms of the child's capacity to read.
5. To develop an awareness of the extent of new reading materials.
6. To conserve teacher efforts in orientation to new materials.

*General suggestions*

1. Read the manuals of materials mentioned above.
2. Discover the sections and parts and determine how they are interrelated.
3. Know what is used by teachers and by pupils.
4. Know the purpose of the kit, lab, or basal series.

5. Know the orientation procedures.
6. Know the evaluation procedures.
7. Know the record-keeping procedures as they relate to teachers and pupils.
8. Conceptualize the classroom organizational procedures.

*Group sharing suggestions*

1. Give classmates an overview of the structure of the resource in such a manner that they will not have to take unreasonable time in becoming oriented to the resource.
2. Show parts of the kit.
3. Show relation of parts to parts; e.g., the feedback (answering) provisions and other sequential phases.
4. Demonstrate the crucial skills, games, or procedures which seem most valuable to know.
5. Allude to the purposes outlined for this guide.
6. Provide for an equitable opportunity to present portions of the resource to the class.
7. Display the various materials.
8. Provide a synopsis of any related research which demonstrates the effectiveness of the program.

The instructor's role during the sharing of the core knowledge gained from the student reports is to

1. Stimulate recognition of resource and basal reader overlap in purposes and to recognize their different strategies.
2. Raise questions as to the validity of the resources as supported by research.
3. Point out how BRP can be strengthened by the incorporation and modification of procedures through the addition of materials.
4. Identify the unique possibilities of the resources for individualization.
5. Note the strengths and weaknesses of resources.
6. Identify local uses of the materials for class observations and demonstrations.

The preceding activities are culminated with the illustrated survey of Reading Resource Characteristics to establish their utility in reading programs.

Other important phases of course content are similarly related to BRP structures to give content the type of meaningfulness thought to be transferable to the teaching of reading in public schools.

# Reading Resource Characteristics

**Response Characteristics**

Directions: Check and evaluate each program with the following qualitative responses

Y = Yes, indicates the program contains this.

YN = Yes and No, indicates the program may contain this.

N = No, indicates the program does not contain this characteristic.

Column headers (programs): SRA Reading Labs · Skill Text · ITA · PLDK · New Practice Readers · Mills – LMT · Hooked on Books · The Teacher – S.A. Warner · Clinic Kit – Webster/McGraw Hill · SRA – RFU · Chandler Series

| Response | SRA Reading Labs | Skill Text | ITA | PLDK | New Practice Readers | Mills – LMT | Hooked on Books | The Teacher – S.A. Warner | Clinic Kit – Webster/McGraw Hill | SRA – RFU | Chandler Series | Characteristic |
|---|---|---|---|---|---|---|---|---|---|---|---|---|
| Y / YN / N | | | | | | | | | | | | A. Provides for heavy emphasis on auditory discrimination |
| Y / YN / N | | | | | | | | | | | | B. Recommended *highly* for the culturally deprived |
| Y / YN / N | | | | | | | | | | | | C. Depends *highly* on the teacher for guidance |
| Y / YN / N | | | | | | | | | | | | D. Provides for quick feedback, independent of the teacher |
| Y / YN / N | | | | | | | | | | | | E. Has multilevel design and is useable in one grade level |
| Y / YN / N | | | | | | | | | | | | F. Provides for pre- or post-testing or both |
| Y / YN / N | | | | | | | | | | | | G. Has a major emphasis on developing meaning or critical reading |
| Y / YN / N | | | | | | | | | | | | H. Has a major emphasis on developing meaning or critical reading |
| Y / YN / N | | | | | | | | | | | | I. Encourages self-motivation/self-direction; makes independent self-improvement highly possible |
| Y / YN / N | | | | | | | | | | | | J. Stresses listening skill development via special lessons or units |
| Y / YN / N | | | | | | | | | | | | K. Provides for heavy emphasis on visual discrimination |
| Y / YN / N | | | | | | | | | | | | L. Intended for upper grades or junior high. |

Name:

## Summary

Recent developments of reading behavioral objectives contribute much to the development of reading course content structure. Notably, the objectives of the Wisconsin Prototypic Program become more meaningful as students engage in discovery type experiences. From the posture taken in this paper, it appears that reading content should stress that "the structure of knowledge—its connectedness and derivations that make one idea follow another—is the proper emphasis in education" as Bruner (11) emphasizes. Hopefully, the strategies here will help teachers utilize the best of new knowledge and materials for the improvement of reading instruction.

## References

1. Aaron, Ira E. "What Teachers and Prospective Teachers Know About Phonic Generalizations," *Journal of Educational Research*, 53 (May 1960), 323-330.

2. Austin, Mary C., and Coleman Morrison. *The First R: The Harvard Report on Reading in Elementary Schools.* New York: Macmillan, 1963.

3. Ausubel, David P. "The Use of Advance Organizers in the Learning and Retention of Meaningful Verbal Material," *Journal of Educational Psychology*, 51 (1960), 267-272.

4. Ausubel, David P. "In Defense of Verbal Learning," *Educational Theory*, 11 (January 1961), 15-25.

5. Bailey, M. H. "Utility of Phonic Generalizations in Grades One through Six," *Reading Teacher*, 20 (Fall 1967), 412-418.

6. Barton, Allen, and David Wilder. "The Columbia-Carnegie Study of Reading Research and Its Communication—An Interim Report," in J. Allen Figurel (Ed.), *Challenge and Experiment in Reading*, Proceedings of the International Reading Association, 7, 1962. New York: Scholastic Magazines, 170-176.

7. Betts, Emmett A. *Foundations of Reading Instruction.* New York: American Book Company, 1957.

8. Betts, Emmett A. "Structure in the Reading Program," *Elementary English*, March 1965, 238-242.

9. Brown, Grace M. *Letters, Sounds, and Words.* San Francisco: San Francisco City University Book Store, 1966.

10. Brown, Grace M., and Alice B. Cottrell. *California Phonics Survey: Manual.* Monterey, California: California Test Bureau, 1963.

11. Bruner, Jerome. *On Knowing.* Cambridge, Massachusetts: Harvard University Press, 1962.

12. Burmeister, Lou E. "An Evaluation of the Inductive and Deductive Group Approaches to Teaching Selected Word Analysis Generalizations to

Disabled Readers in Eighth and Ninth Grades," Research and Development Center for Learning and Reeducation, University of Wisconsin, Madison, 1966.

13. Burton, William H., and Joseph Ilika. "Some Arguments About Reading," *Education*, 84 (March 1964), 387-392.

14. Clymer, Theodore. "The Utility of Phonic Generalizations in the Primary Grades," *Reading Teacher*, 16 (January 1963), 252-258.

15. Cordts, Anna D. *Phonics for the Reading Teacher.* New York: Holt, Rinehart and Winston, 1965.

16. Cordts, Anna D. "The Phonetics of Phonics," *Reading Teacher*, 9 (December 1955), 81-84.

17. Cottrell, Alice B. "A Group Test for Ascertaining Ability in Phonetic Analysis Among College Students," *Dissertation Abstracts*, 18, 1794. Ann Arbor, Michigan: University Microfilms, 1957.

18. Eman, R. "Usefulness of Phonic Generalizations Above the Primary Grades," *Reading Teacher*, 20 (February 1967), 419-425.

19. Farinella, John Thomas. "An Appraisal of Teacher Knowledge of Phonetic Analysis and Structural Analysis," unpublished doctoral dissertation, University of Connecticut. *Dissertation Abstracts*, 21, 1960, 1805.

20. Gagon, Glen Scott. "A Diagnostic Study of the Phonic Abilities of Elementary Teachers in the State of Utah," *Dissertation Abstracts*, 60, 6256. Ann Arbor, Michigan: University Microfilms, 1960.

21. Henriksen, Emmaline B. "An Analysis of Teacher Knowledge of Word Recognition Skills," *Dissertation Abstracts*, 69, 9492. Ann Arbor, Michigan: University Microfilms, 1968.

22. Ilika, Joseph. "The Extent of Teacher Preparation and the Development of Word Analysis Knowledge Among Teacher Education Students," *Journal of the Reading Specialist*, 10 (March 1971), 124-127.

23. Ilika, Joseph. "Phonic Skills of Teacher Education Students and Teachers," *Multidisciplinary Aspects of College—Adult Reading*, Seventeenth Yearbook of the National Reading Conference, 1967.

24. Ilika, Joseph. "A Second Report on the Phonic Skills of Teachers and Teacher Education Students," in George B. Schick and Merrill M. May (Eds.), *The Psychology of Reading Behavior*, Eighteenth Yearbook of the National Reading Conference. Milwaukee: National Reading Conference, 1969, 168-175.

25. Miller, James G. "The Information Explosion: Implications for Teaching," *Journal of the National Association of Women Deans and Counselors*, 27 (Winter 1963), 54-59.

26. Mink, Oscar G. "Experience and Cognitive Structure," *Journal of Research in Science Teaching*, 2 (1964), 196-203.

27. Morrison, Coleman, A. J. Harris, and I. T. Auerbach. *After Effects of Staff Participation in a Reading Research Project: A Follow-up Study of the*

*Craft Project.* City University of New York, Office of Research and Evaluation, 1968.

28. Serlin, Janet. "Are Methods a Madness?" *Reading Newsreport,* 4 (April 1970), 22-26.

29. Shannon, M. "The Measurement of Phonetic Understandings Relevant to the Teaching of Reading," unpublished doctoral dissertation, Harvard University, 1959.

30. Spache, George D. "Materials Explosion," in J. Allen Figurel (Ed.), *Vistas in Reading,* 1966 Proceedings Volume 11, Part 1. Newark, Delaware: International Reading Association, 1967.

31. Spache, George D., and Evelyn B. Spache. *Reading in the Elementary School.* New York: Allyn and Bacon, 1969.

32. Staiger, Ralph C. "How Are Basal Readers Used?" *Elementary English,* January 1958, 44-46.

33. Stauffer, Russell G. *Directing Reading Maturity as a Cognitive Process.* London: Harper and Row, 1969.

34. Templeton, A. B. *Reading Disorders in the United States: The Secretary's (HEW) Advisory Committee on Dyslexia and Related Reading Disorders,* 1969.

35. Wilson, Robert M., and MaryAnne Hall. *Programmed Word Attack for Teachers.* Columbus, Ohio: Charles E. Merrill, 1968.

# DEVELOPING AND EVALUATING COMPETENCIES FOR TEACHERS OF READING

*Sandra Jo Hornick*
*Kent State University*

There have been many models of field experience, competency based programs in teacher education in the past few years. There recently has been voiced a concern that prospective elementary classroom teachers of reading should begin early to develop the professional competencies of diagnosing children's needs and abilities and prescribing the kinds of experiences and materials that best meet these needs in helping children become successful readers. The abilities to diagnose and prescribe can best be developed, in this writer's opinion, through work with children in actual classroom situations under the close supervision and guidance of classroom teachers and college personnel.

With these observations in mind, the writer has been engaged in an ongoing action research project to attempt to identify and develop a set of sufficiently broad competencies in the preparation of such prospective reading teachers. This action research of determining and attempting to evaluate such competencies is being implemented within a language arts methods course for which a student receives seven hours credit for a ten week quarter. Although the writer is concentrating on the area of reading for this paper, competencies are also being developed in the teaching of listening, speaking, and writing within the course structure as well.

Twenty to forty junior students per quarter who have had basic courses in child growth and development and learning theories take part in the program prior to student teaching. Students are screened for the program by personal interview and assigned one per classroom situation to work (two hours per day, two to four days per week during the quarter) in public elementary schools to which they are bussed. The remaining one to two days per week are spent on campus in lectures, small group sessions, instructional media production, videotape analyses of lessons, and research for lessons and activities. For the most part, classrooms being used have multibasal reading programs at the primary levels and individualized reading programs at the intermediate levels. For many of the participants, this is their initial experience with children in more than a one-to-one tutorial situation.

Students developing the competencies are evaluated through pencil and paper tests; observations recorded on checklists by the teacher and by the writer; analyses of videotaped demonstration lessons with children; and student development, implementation, and analyses of lessons and activities under the guidance of the college professor and recorded in notebooks. Successful completion of a competency could also be measured by: 1) the student's ability to recognize why a lesson may not have been entirely successful, 2) the student's ability to make suggestions for ways of improving the lesson to help children achieve the behavioral objectives involved, and 3) the student's ability to follow up with a successful experience with the children on another occasion when the competency would be worked on again.

In addition, students are involved in text related activities on campus which explore various reading programs and approaches and the advantages and limitations of each.

## Reading Competencies Identified and Measured

The following eleven competencies which the writer has identified for reading instruction represent only a portion of possible competencies that could be considered. Choices were made on the basis of the writer's knowledge of reading instruction, instructional tasks of elementary teachers, and the limitations of time within a quarter period of ten weeks. Some omitted competencies for effective teaching of reading are within the affective domain and at the present time are most difficult to define in terms of accountability.

1. *Student will successfully pass with a grade of 80 percent or above a word recognition skills test consisting of word recognition skills knowledge and application of this knowledge.* This competency is measured by an objective item and short essay pencil and paper test. Pretesting, practical application in teaching situations, and posttesting are the patterns to be pursued, for the writer has found that students learn generalizations in phonetic analysis or structural analysis quickly, but do not crystallize concepts of application of these generalizations until the intervention of some time in a practical setting. Students then know what the word recognition skills are and,

in fulfilling the requirements for Competency 3, see the many approaches in process that might be needed in teaching children these skills. Successful completion of Competency 1 is needed before attempting Competency 3.

> A sample test item: *Objective*—auditory discrimination of the initial consonant *b*. *Background*—The lesson has been under way. The teacher is pronouncing pairs of words and asking the children to indicate whether the words begin alike or differently. *Teacher*—I will pronounce two words. Tell me if the words have the same beginning sound or not *(ball-tall; ball-tall)*. *Child*—Same. What would you do as the teacher in responding?

2. *Student will successfully pass with a grade of 80 percent or above a comprehension skills test consisting of knowledge of comprehension levels and skills and application of this knowledge.* This competency is measured in the same manner as Competency 1. The same pattern of pretesting, practical experience, posttesting will be followed for testing knowledge of comprehension levels and skills. Successful completion of this competency is necessary for successful completion of Competencies 6 and 11 soon to be described.

> A sample test item: After children have finished reading a selection on moths and butterflies, how would you aid them in organizing and recalling details that support how moths and butterflies are similar and different? Would you have them outline, list, classify? Describe the activity you would use and why.

3. *Student will develop a word recognition skills diagnostic survey to use with children at the student's assigned participation/ teaching level. Student will administer the survey test to a small group of children, determine their needs, and plan lessons or activities to teach the skills needed using a multisensory approach. Children will successfully pass a posttest after the instruction with a score of eighty percent or better. Student will analyze the results.* An observation checklist is used by the writer to evaluate the teaching aspect of this competency as well as a checklist that is used to analyze the development, implementation, and analysis of both the testing instruments and the lesson plans. Areas that are evaluated include: inclusion of word recognition skills appropriate to the age and ability level of each child, validity and reliability of the test used so that children do not guess the correct responses, completeness of recording and analysis of test results, correlation of the results of the testing and the kinds of lessons planned to teach needed skills, provisions for varied learning styles in planning lessons, and amount and kind of improvement on the part of the children after instruction.

4. *Student will identify the instructional reading level(s) of one to three children in his classroom through the use of an informal reading inventory which he has constructed.*

5. *Student will select reading materials at the instructional level of at least one of the children in the test in number 4 and, taking specific behavioral objectives, teach a directed reading lesson if the material being used is of a basal nature or plan and implement a conference for children working within an individualized reading program. Student planning, implementation, and analysis of the lesson or conference will be evaluated in terms of the children's success in meeting the behavioral objectives of the lesson plan or conference.* Points to be considered in the evaluation of competencies four and five are: accuracy and feasibility of testing instrument, analysis of data, basis of interpretation of test data, selection of reading materials at child's instructional level, appropriateness of lesson or conference objectives and planning, organization of conference. A few students compared the results of their test instruments and the results obtained from using commercially prepared instruments and found a high level of reliability. Observation of the lesson or conference and analysis of the write-up of the test and analysis of test results serve as the basis for evaluation of the successful completion of these competencies.

6. *Student will develop questions on the literal, interpretative, and critical/creative levels of comprehension for a story or article. Children will read the story or article silently under student guidance. Student will analyze children's responses to discussion questions to determine the cognitive levels of response represented.* Using Bloom's *Taxonomy of Educational Objectives: Cognitive Domain* as a basis for determining levels of cognition, both the students and the writer developed a scale to record children's responses by initials to identify each child and by a numerical system to record levels of questions. Students were observed and they analyzed their own discussion periods after they were audiotaped. Presently, work is being done to help students formulate questions in the affective domain as well.

7. *Student will develop an experience story with a small group of children at the primary level, or with one child who needs help with reading in the intermediate grades, and will record accurately the children's contributions. Student will then analyze the story for possible reading instruction in word or letter recognition skills, comprehension, and/or vocabulary development. Student will justify his choice of instructional work based on his knowledge of the children's needs and abilities and knowledge of content of the skills*

*areas for the children's levels.* Videotaping of lessons, observational checklists, and analyses of notebook write-ups are again applied to evaluate this competency. Points considered are: is story developed correctly (discussion, choice of topic, recording, or development of writing effort); is story fully analyzed for instructional or follow-up purposes; and do follow-up lessons build upon the story writing experience?

8. *Student will develop an interest inventory to use with a group of children. Student will use the data from this inventory to plan classroom activities to encourage more interest in books. Student will later determine any changes in children's interest in reading by observation, discussion with children, and by notation of preferences for reading when choices can be made.* Students in the primary grades used more informal methods of inventorying interests than students in the intermediate grades. All inventory methods were evaluated in terms of appropriateness and feasibility.

9. *Student will read and share stories with the whole class to develop a literary understanding such as the recognition of similarity of themes in several stories. Children, after discussion and instruction, will use their understanding of theme to develop their own story plots.* Students, depending on the literary understanding they wish to develop with children, also use oral situations to determine the children's grasp of the understanding. Evaluative instruments used: checklist to observe lesson or activity for developing literary understanding, and checklist to analyze, with student, the children's understanding through their written or oral work.

10. *Student will develop a checklist of oral reading skills and abilities for the children in his classroom. Student will administer the checklist to an individual, a small group, or the whole class. Student will develop, on the basis of the data as guidelines, at least one lesson or activity for oral reading. Evaluation will be on the basis of children's ability to meet the behavioral objectives of the plan.* In most instances, meeting the objectives meant that the children worked to improve oral reading skills. General oral reading areas included word recognition, fluency, use of voice, posture, and interpretation of material. The same kinds of instruments were used again by the writer in evaluating this competency.

11. *Student will take a child's text in one of the content areas and develop a study guide for effective reading of one chapter, using aids such as captions and titles, vocabulary development, and guided silent reading questions. Children will, after instruction with the study guide, pass a written test on the content of the chapter.* Points that were considered in evaluating the student's fulfillment of this

competency centered on choice of materials, development of study guide, and evidence, when tested on the material, that children learned from such guidance in content area reading. Also, the effectiveness of the test as it correlated with the study guide was considered.

In attempting to identify and measure competencies in teaching reading, the writer finds that students do begin to form a picture of the total involvement of children and teacher in the reading process. They do become acquainted with many aspects of reading instruction and they do begin to analyze their own strengths and weaknesses upon which they will continue to work through their experiences in student teaching and in the professional world as well. This, then, is a beginning.

Additional work continues on evaluation instruments for children's evaluation of students, teacher's evaluation of the student, and student self-evaluation. Space and time limitations prevent further discussion here; however, as with the other instruments being worked with and refined by the writer, samples can be shared with those interested in teacher education programs of this kind.

# SUPERVISING THE EVALUATION OF COMPETENCIES

*Joan B. Nelson*
*University of Pittsburgh*

While there is still considerable controversy regarding the efficacy and merit of a competency based approach to teacher education, the advantages of the competency approach seem to outweigh the disadvantages. Indeed, most of the disadvantages cited by critics can be as readily applied to traditional programs as to competency based programs. The advantages, on the other hand, are inherent in the approach.

Since our major interest is in the evaluation of teacher education programs, especially for the training of reading personnel, let us consider the characteristics and advantages of a competency based approach and then implications for evaluation of such a program.

The Department of Reading and Language Arts at the University of Pittsburgh has been involved in the development and implementation of a competency based program for the training of reading specialists and reading supervisors. Based on experiences in developing this program, certain distinct advantages may be seen as clearly related to program characteristics. The following is a list of the characteristics of a competency based program and the advantages growing out of each:

1. *Competencies are derived from professional role expectancies.*

   - Definitions of role expectancies may be gleaned from surveys of school superintendents, principals, supervisors, reading personnel, teachers, students, professors of education, professional organizations, and parents. Competency requirements describe behaviors that are either presently required or are seen as appropriate to the role.

   - A much broader input regarding necessary competencies allows the ultimate consumer of these competencies a voice in defining them. This has not been the case where professors of education, some of whom are out of touch with the real world of school districts, have taken the full responsibility for defining course objectives.

2. *Competency requirements for a given program are explicitly stated and made public.*

   - While a competency based approach does not insure that a program is good, it makes it easier to tell when program goals are explicit (2).
   - Students are aided in making judgments as to whether they wish to participate in the program and in knowing what is expected of them if they enter it.
   - Instructors are aided in making judgments about what instructional resources and activities to include.
   - Employers are aided in making judgments about what competencies program graduates can be expected to possess and whether these competencies are appropriate to the specific employment role.

3. *Assessment of competency is based on performance of criterion behaviors which manifest the competency.*

   - The emphasis is on performance rather than a set of credentials or an accumulation of knowledge.
   - Evaluation focuses not so much on what the student knows, but how he applies what he knows in an actual teaching situation.

4. *The student's rate of progress is determined by demonstrated competency rather than by time or course completion.*

   - Competencies may be preassessed, allowing the student to concentrate on areas in which he is not competent.
   - Students take responsibility for learning and self-evaluation.
   - The instructor becomes a facilitator of learning rather than a dispenser of knowledge.
   - Much greater individualization is possible.

5. *Competency based education is field oriented.*

   - Competencies developed in the program can be demonstrated and evaluated in a school setting.
   - The base of evaluation is extended to include school personnel.
   - Program objectives can be reality tested.

Many other characteristics and advantages may be listed, but those presented provide a basis for the major thrust of this paper which is to explore the logistics of supervising the evaluation of competencies. A competency based program to be workable must develop systems and strategies for assessment and accountability. The systems and strategies presently in development at the University of Pittsburgh will be described as examples of management possibilities. It should be made clear, however, that this approach is only one of many possible approaches that may be appropriate depending upon the constraints of the situation (e.g., the amount of support provided, the practicality of field-site contracts, the necessity of communication with the institution in terms of course credits).

To begin with, it should be recognized that there is more than a semantic difference between competency based and performance based education. A competency represents a potential for many different performances in a variety of settings. A performance is an actualization of the potential, but it is the development of the potential that is crucial. A performance may be practiced and perfected without acquisition of the knowledges and understandings that are required for a competency. A competency is made up of knowledges, understandings, attitudes, and skills. It is manifested in performances which may be defined as criterion behaviors. There are, however, a variety of performances that may manifest the same competency. There is no need for the student to perform every possible criterion behavior in order to ensure the accomplishment of the competency requirement.

Given this philosophy, it is possible to list competency requirements in fairly broad behavioral terms. The student may then choose among various criterion behaviors at several levels to demonstrate the competency.

Let us use as an example one of the competencies that might be listed in a program for reading specialists: *The student is able to choose, administer, and interpret a reading test that is appropriate for a given situation.*

The competency statement assumes certain knowledges, understandings, skills, and attitudes. There are various criterion behaviors that might be used to manifest the competency as well as a variety of proximate objectives and criterion behaviors to reach it. A whole unit or module might be developed to implement the accomplishment of this single competency objective.

## Levels of Competency

Competencies may also be assessed by performances at several levels: preparation level, simulation level, and application level. Using the same competency example we can follow through the various levels.

*The preparation level.* The objectives at this level emphasize the knowledges, understandings, and attitudes that are required for the development of a competency. For example, the student might attend minilectures or study textbooks or test manuals for knowledge on the principals of testing, reliability and validity, objectivity and standardization. He might then take part in a discussion of these concepts or take a pencil and paper test to demonstrate the accomplishment of the objective. (Many traditional teacher education programs operate only at the preparation level.)

*The simulation level.* The objectives at this level emphasize the skills and abilities that are required for the development of a competency. The student might study test manuals to acquire the ability to administer a given test; he might then administer the test to several of his colleagues to gain practice and feedback on his performance and then administer the test to a child in clinic or field-site under the close supervision of an instructor. (Some traditional programs provide experiences at the simulation level.)

*The application level.* The objectives at this level focus on the demonstration and validation of competencies in a real school setting with school personnel and university supervisors as resources. The student is expected to choose an appropriate test in a given situation, administer the test according to the test manual and interpret the results of the test to the child's teacher or the supervisor. (This field evaluation is peculiar to competency based programs.)

## Types of Objectives

The concept of assessment of objectives at the levels described suggests that we must also be concerned with kinds of objectives. It is not enough to say behavioral objectives; it is also necessary to recognize that behavioral objectives come in an assortment of criterion types according to desired outcomes. Houston and Howsam (*1*) list five types of objectives broadly defined as follows:

1. *Cognitive objectives*, which specify knowledges and understandings to be demonstrated by the learner. These can be assessed by verbal interaction or paper and pencil test. (We sometimes forget that performance on a test is indeed a behavior. Example: The student answers a question indicating knowledge of reliability or validity in connection with tests.)

2. *Performance objectives*, which specify skills and abilities to be demonstrated by the learner. These are generally assessed by the student's doing something. (Example: Student administers a test.)

3. *Consequence objectives*, which specify the consequences of the learner's performance. (Example: The student administers a test and is evaluated on the effect of his testing on his pupil, e.g., whether the pupil responded without obvious hostility or anxiety.)

4. *Affective objectives*, which specify the attitudes, feelings, beliefs, and values of the student. While change in affective behavior is difficult to assess, no program for training of reading personnel can afford to neglect affective dimensions. (Example: A change in the student's attitude toward standardized testing as an effective means of assessing reading achievement may be one of the most important objectives in the unit.)

5. *Exploratory objectives*, which specify experiences which hold promise for significant learnings but lack definition of desired outcomes. (Example: The student may be asked to visit a ghetto neighborhood.) While no specific outcome may be expected, the experience may lead to the definition of other objectives that may be meaningful. (Example: The student may realize that he is unprepared to cope with children from cultural subgroups or that standardized tests are sometimes biased against children who use nonstandard dialects.)

The evaluation of performances to demonstrate competency looms as a tremendous task even when competencies are explicitly stated, using different types of objectives for varying levels of performance. Just as the approach responds to differences in student rate of learning by making progress in the program contingent upon demonstrated competency rather than time or course completion, it should also respond to individual differences in learning style by providing a variety of learning experiences and many options. There must also be choices among criterion behaviors used to demonstrate competency.

It seems obvious that evaluation of competencies is inextricably bound to the total development of a competency based program. It is part and parcel of the process from beginning to end and at every step in between. It requires the development of preassessment tools, instructional packages, protocol and training materials, and, most important, appropriate settings for the preparation, practice, simulation, demonstration, and validation of competencies.

## Preassessment Tools

The individualized nature of competency based education requires the development of preassessment tools. If a student already possesses certain competencies he/she should have the opportunity of demonstrating the competency to eliminate the necessity of engaging in redundant activities. In traditional programs the student is usually required to sit through lectures or repetitive learning experiences because there is no occasion ahead of time to demonstrate his competency.

Preassessment tools may be developed at each level, such as a paper and pencil test for knowledge at the preparation level, the development of a sample lesson plan in response to a videotaped situation at the simulation level, and a field test at the application level.

## Instructional Packages

Optional learning experiences and criterion behaviors may be provided through the development of instructional packages for the accomplishment of certain objectives that lend themselves to this treatment. Packages may be designed for both group and individual use. They should probably include 1) *objectives*, stated as behaviors; 2) *preassessments*, allowing opportunity to demonstrate competency ahead of time; 3) *selected readings*, for knowledge and understanding; 4) *suggested learning activities*, for reinforcement of knowledge and development of skills; and 5) *criterion behaviors*, to show ways of demonstrating the accomplishment of the objectives.

Instructional packages should be designed to include self-evaluation, peer evaluation, instructor evaluation, and, finally, field evaluation. The instructor's role in the process is that of resource person, facilitator of learning, and coevaluator. The student is expected to take considerable responsibility for his own learning. His progress in that learning can be readily monitored by use of student journals in which students, instructors, and field personnel sign off on activities engaged in and criterion behaviors demonstrated. The terminal competency-behaviors demonstrated in the culminating field experience act as the ultimate criteria for all proximate experiences and behaviors developed during program experiences.

## Protocol Materials

Protocol materials may be a part of instructional packages or may be used by instructors who wish to provide simulation of classroom behaviors to facilitate the development of interpretive competencies. Videotaped, audiotaped, or printed material may be developed to show behaviors that portray concepts in teaching and learning. They may be used to initiate discussion, to stimulate learning, or to test responses in the form of criterion behaviors. For example, a videotaped film sequence of the interaction of a classroom teacher with the children in a reading group may be used 1) to initiate discussion of questioning strategies used by the teacher, 2) to provide examples of types of questions used by teachers, and 3) to evaluate student ability to recognize and categorize types of questions.

The development of protocol materials can facilitate many instructional goals where simulation of actual classroom setting is desired.

## Clinic and Field Settings

Probably the most important feature of a competency based program is the development and management of the field settings that are required for the demonstration and validation of competencies. The traditional student teaching model is totally inappropriate.

*Clinic.* A clinic setting must be organized and managed so that students may demonstrate competencies under the close supervision of experienced clinicians. Clinic clients should never be used in guinea pig fashion. The student should have the opportunity to observe, practice, and refine his skill before he validates his experience in a real situation. Videotaped testing and tutoring sessions may be used for observation and feedback. Peers may be used for practice as well as for feedback and evaluation. In his work with clients the student should operate in a team arrangement with an experienced reading clinician.

*Field site.* The culminating activity for any good program must be the practice, demonstration, and validation of competencies in a real school setting. The student must have the opportunity to take part in the conceptualization, planning, implementation, and evaluation of a total school reading program. The program must provide the management processes wherein the student may demonstrate his competencies within that framework.

The Department of Reading and Language Arts at the University of Pittsburgh has developed a unique field site model which is operating in various stages of development at a number of school districts in the Pittsburgh area. The school district contracts with the department for a resident contingency team consisting of a faculty member (one day a week), a doctoral student (two days a week), and two supervisory level students (three days a week). Ideally, team members are all experienced reading specialists or supervisors. The arrangement provides benefits in both directions. The school district acquires built-in reading specialists who aid teachers in diagnosis, remediation, development of teaching skills, and inservice programs. The department uses the school district as a field setting for students who may then work under the constant supervision of the resident team. The demonstration of competencies becomes a part of the ongoing team process. This is a far cry from the traditional student teaching model where a "circuit rider" supervisor may appear once a week to observe student teaching behaviors. Students in the Pittsburgh program are part of a team which is constantly available as a resource.

It is very clear that each of the topics and subtopics mentioned could be expanded into a presentation or a series of presentations. The logistics of supervising the evaluation of competencies is an issue of continuing concern for educators who value a competency based approach.

## Summary

It is not enough in a competency based program to explicate objectives, criterion behaviors, and instructional resources. Given the nature and characteristics of the approach it is essential to develop systems and strategies that allow for individualization of instruction, accommodation to both rate and style of learning, and accommodation to the constraints of the institutional setting. Vital to any competency based teacher education program is the development of preassessment tools, instructional packages, training and protocol materials, and, most important of all, clinical settings and field sites with support personnel for the demonstration and validation of competencies. The logistics of such a program require that students take considerable responsibility for their own learning, that instructors act as facilitators of learning rather than dispensers of knowledge, and that the evaluation process include student self-evaluation, peer evaluation, instructor evaluation, and field personnel evaluation.

## References

1. Houston, R., and B. Howsam. *Competency Based Teacher Education.* Chicago: Science Research Associates, 1972.

2. Schmieder, A. *Competency Based Education: The State of the Scene.* Washington, D.C.: AACTE, 1973.

# EXPERIMENTAL PROGRAMS IN ELEMENTARY SCHOOL CLASSROOMS

*Robert M. Wilson*
*University of Maryland*
*and*
*Marcia M. Barnes*
*Montgomery County, Maryland*

Professors obtain ideas from a variety of sources. Research journals, books, students, and school visitations are common sources of ideas for educational innovation. However, the charge is often made that professors dwell too much on theory which is not practical or is too difficult to implement. The complaint usually ends with a suggestion that the professor return to the classroom for a year to see how it really is. This suggestion has much to offer, but the reality of the situation is that return visits do not occur. The excuse usually offered is that the professor's job demands constant attention to student advising, committee work, research writing, and other projects and leaves no time for other things.

But theory does run into difficulty when attempts are made at implementation. The suggested theory may be impractical, may run into difficulty when attempted over a long period of time, or may be in need of modification for implementation.

The purpose of this paper is to present a way out of the dilemma; a way which is both practical and desirable and which benefits all involved—the professors, the teacher implementers, and the children.

## One Solution

Identify a school in which several teachers are willing to work with the professor to implement theories of education. The professor will work in that school one morning a week helping to implement his theories, evaluating the results, adjusting the implementation, and reevaluating.

Planning time is needed to meet with the teachers to work out the implementation scheme and to acquaint teachers with the theory. Biweekly conferences outside of school hours can be arranged to accomplish the necessary team effort.

As theories are placed into action, the professor can conduct demonstration lessons, set controls for data collection, assist the teacher with explanations for parents and school officials, assist with long term adjustments, and be responsible for evaluation. The teacher assumes the basic responsibility for the day-to-day work with children. He makes minor adjustments, suggests modifications, and assists with evaluation and planning.

## In Practice

The writers are currently implementing a program following these ideas. They have selected five innovations, from a list of fifteen, for examples of how the system works.

1. *The theory.* Children learn best when they feel accepted, loved, and needed in the classroom.

   *Professor's suggestion.* Each week feature one child as the personality of the week. Place a picture of him in a designated spot in the classroom and have other children write short statements about what they like best about the child.

   *Teacher's implementation.* Set aside bulletin board space in the room. Select one child a week, and on Monday post his picture on the bulletin board. Have cards or pieces of paper available for writing and thumb tacks for each child to attach his statement. The first personality child in the writers' group became so excited that he removed all the cards about him while his teacher was at lunch, and packed them up to take home and show his mother. The second child insisted that his mother come to school that day to see the display. This gimmick has definitely encouraged each child to look for positive attributes in others and to feel good about himself.

2. *The theory.* Children learn best when they are involved in the selection of what they are to learn and can pace their own learning.

   *Professor's suggestion.* Have the children in the room select their own spelling words from the reading and writing they are doing in other areas of the curriculum. Then, let them contract with the teacher for the number of words they think they can learn in a given week.

   *Teacher's implementation.* Have a class list to which children add words of their own interest from Monday through Friday. On the following Monday, give a practice test to determine which words on the list may already be in the child's spelling vocabulary. Each child then picks (possibly with some guidance from the teacher) the number of words he would like to learn from the words he misspelled. This procedure is suggested to help children become more involved and enthusiastic and realize their own potential and strive to reach it. After the child has selected the words which he will learn during the week, his second step is to identify a method or methods by which he will study these words. Initially, the children develop a list of "different ways to study a word," i.e., write words in a sentence or trace. After sufficient time has been given to ensure that the children are familiar with the various techniques and are able to utilize each to their advantage, they select the method(s) which they will use while learning their words. The children keep a record of which method(s) they use during the week. At the end of the week, this record enables the teacher and the children to determine whether the method(s) used were helpful (see Appendix B). With the possible exception of one child, the writers noticed no feelings of anxiety or frustration due to failure or boredom.

3. *The theory.* Children learn best if they can have a choice in selecting with whom they will work.

*Professor's suggestion.* Assign children to reading groups, if you wish, but allow them to read in any other group that they choose. In other words, poor readers can choose to read in fast reading groups as well as in their own.

*Teacher's implementation.* Establish two days a week for open groups, two for closed groups, and one for individual reading. Modify the professor's suggestion for open groups everyday 1) to introduce the children gradually to the change to be sure they use the idea to advantage, 2) to give the teacher an opportunity to concentrate on children with similar skill needs, and 3) to make the opportunity not routine so children might look forward to it. A problem occurred in implementing the open groups because children in the lower groups were anxious to read in groups where the material was too difficult. The professor suggested grouping several slow readers with a "good" reader who would read aloud. As more children began to visit and as paired reading became more prevalent, the children began to feel more comfortable and began to look forward to the opportunity to visit another group.

4. *The theory.* Children learn best when instruction is diagnostic. Commercially prepared materials are not suitable for teaching skills in reading. The skills a child needs may not be in the skills section of the manual.

*Professor's suggestion.* Assess children's skills strengths and weaknesses early in the school year. Then use skill grouping designed to meet the children's strengths and weaknesses; these skill groups need not relate to reading level.

*Teacher's implementation.* At the start of this school year, the teacher and professor administered the Botel Word Opposites Test and the Botel Phonics Test to the class. They checked and analyzed each child and drew up a profile chart of skill areas. Children who were "poor" in several areas were given an auditory perception test to determine whether their problem could be lack of ability to hear sounds correctly. Results showed the possiblity that two children had this difficulty. Meanwhile, skill groups were established in the other areas of strengths and weaknesses, and a general review was given for the areas where the children showed a "fair" response. The professor suggested activities which he felt might aid the children in these groups. At the end of eight weeks, the children were retested in order to see areas of either adequate or poor progress (see Appendix A) so that something could be done about the weak areas. The teacher wrote, "I can see this as being my fault entirely as I probably did not develop these problem areas fully enough. I can surmise that a reason might be that the first test showed several skill areas weaknesses, so I may have tried to teach too much too fast. I hate to think of how many months it could have taken me to discover so many details. Maybe it would have been too late for some."

5. *The theory.* Children learn more when they evaluate their own performance than they do when the teacher evaluates it.

*Professor's suggestion.* For all activities which are assigned for independent work, have the children evaluate their efforts and their product prior to turning in the work to the teacher. They can self-evaluate with smiling or frowning faces, comments, or phrases and sentences. The teacher should help the children develop realistic self-evaluation techniques by commenting upon the papers. Conferences may be necessary in extreme cases.

*Teacher's implementation.* The teacher reported, "We started in one subject area. To my surprise every child was extremely anxious to know how I evaluated what they had done and almost demanded immediate feedback. I almost gave up. But then I noticed remarkable improvement. I expanded the idea so that now every child self-evaluates every paper (not tests) prior to handing them to me. Five months into this procedure has resulted in a full two-thirds of the class caring more about their own evaluations than they do about mine. They have moved from very simple evaluations to comments such as 'very good ideas, but the handwriting needs some improvement.' "

Each of the writers' other innovations focuses on the theories of self-selection, self-pacing, and self-correction as effective learning activities. Each also focuses upon the advantages of individualizing instruction.

## Reactions

General reaction is that the program is very effective for the professor, the teacher, and the children. Every professor's suggestion was in need of modification and rethinking. Some typical reactions follow:

*The professor.* My course work on campus has become more relevant to what is going on in a classroom on a contingency basis. My theories are being supported, but my suggestions for implementing are being adjusted. I can sell my ideas better because I can relate them to what happened yesterday morning instead of ten years ago. I find the teacher cooperative and willing to change, but only when she can feel free to modify and criticize. The project is worth every minute spent so far.

*The teacher.* As a classroom teacher, my everyday concern has been how I can help each individual in a class of twenty-nine or thirty to develop his potential. I have felt frustrated at seeing my most capable student idle while I tried to help the slower students or seeing the slower students become frustrated while I tried to encourage the rest. I had some ideas but I didn't know how to implement them in a way that I could be assured of some success. I confronted the professor with my situation and he has visited my classroom regularly and offered many suggestions and ideas. I have appreciated them all because it has given me a real opportunity to do something for more children in the classroom. I have also had the opportunity to try some exciting ideas that other people have tried and found successful. I do not see so many tears or frowns from frustration as I have seen before. I hope we can modify and add to our program as the need arises. The project has been worth every minute for me, also.

*The children.* The pupils have reacted favorably for the most part. Their reactions (pro and con) are in Appendix C.

The children did not react to the skills testing and teaching; they may not really have been aware of what was going on. However, they did react eagerly to the other innovations.

## Summary

Teachers and professors can work together to the mutual benefit of both. More efforts of the type explained in this paper might well eliminate the feelings of unreality connected with methods courses. The cooperative spirit which results from the effort strengthens the bonds between the university and the local schools.

The teacher is now in a position to assist other teachers as they express an interest in what she is doing. She develops confidence through constant interaction with the professor. She works out every detail and then evaluates it.

*See Appendixes A, B, and C on the following pages.*

# Appendix A

| Child | Reading Level | Consonants | Blends | Digraphs | Rhyming Words | Vowels | Auditory Discrimination | Syllabication |
|-------|---------------|------------|--------|----------|---------------|--------|-------------------------|---------------|
| 1 | 6 | G-G | G-G | G-G | G-G | G-G | – | G-G |
| 2 | 6 | G-G | G-G | G-G | G-G | F-F | – | F-G |
| 3 | 5 | G-G | G-G | G-G | G-G | G-G | – | G-G |
| 4 | 5 | G-G | G-G | F-G | G-G | F-G | – | F-G |
| 5 | 4 | G-G | G-G | G-G | G-G | G-G | – | G-G |
| 6 | 4 | F-G | P-P | P-P | G-G | G-G | – | – |
| 7 | 4 | G-G | G-G | G-G | G-G | G-G | – | G-G |
| 8 | 4 | G-G | P-G | P-G | G-G | F-G | – | – |
| 9 | 4 | G-G | F-G | G-G | G-G | F-G | – | – |
| 10 | 3-2 | G-G | G-G | P-G | G-G | G-G | – | – |
| 11 | 3-2 | G-G | G-G | F-G | G-G | F-G | – | – |
| 12 | 3-2 | G-G | G-G | G-G | G-G | G-G | – | F-G |
| 13 | 3-2 | G-G | G-G | G-G | G-G | G-G | – | G-G |
| 14 | 3-2 | G-G | P-G | P-G | G-G | P-G | – | – |
| 15 | 3-2 | G-G | G-G | G-G | G-G | G-G | – | F-G |
| 16 | 3-1 | G-G | P-G | P-G | P-G | P-P | – | – |
| 17 | 3-1 | F-G | G-G | F-G | G-G | G-G | – | – |
| 18 | 3-1 | G-G | F-F | P-G | G-G | F-G | G-G | – |
| 19 | 3-1 | G-G | G-G | G-G | G-G | G-G | – | F-G |
| 20 | 2-2 | G-G | F-G | F-G | F-G | G-G | F-F | – |
| 21 | 2-1 | G-G | F-F | P-G | G-G | F-G | G-G | – |
| 22 | 2-1 | G-G | G-G | G-G | F-G | F-F | G-G | – |
| 23 | 2-1 | G-G | G-G | P-G | P-G | G-G | G-G | – |
| 24 | 1 | F-G | P-F | P-G | P-G | P-G | G-G | – |
| 25 | 1 | G-G | P-G | P-G | G-G | P-G | F-G | – |
| 26 | P | P-P | P-P | P-P | P-P | P-P | P-G | – |

Marked progress can be demonstrated by analyzing the strengths and weaknesses of each child and by adjusting instruction accordingly.

This chart shows several of the benefits of diagnostic teaching. The Reading Level column shows the results of the Botel Reading Inventory, Word Opposites section.

In the other columns are two letters (G-good, F-fair, or P-poor). The first entry under each skill indicates the rating each child received on the second day of school; the second indicates his rating at the end of eight weeks. A dash indicates no testing.

How would you like to be the teacher in a parent conference with child number 14 or 16 or 25?

## Appendix B

| Child | Level | Week One | | | Week Two | | | Week Three | | | Week Four | | | Week Five | | |
|---|---|---|---|---|---|---|---|---|---|---|---|---|---|---|---|---|
| | | P | C | F | P | C | F | P | C | F | P | C | F | P | C | F |
| 1 | 6 | 19 | 29 | 30* | 5 | 18 | 18* | 13 | 22 | 27* | 15 | 24 | 25* | 14 | 24 | 26* |
| 2 | 2-1 | 6 | 11 | 11* | 1 | 9 | 9* | 1 | 6 | 7* | 0 | 6 | 6* | 1 | 10 | 9 |
| 3 | 1 | 2 | 7 | 7* | 1 | 7 | 7* | 3 | 9 | 9* | 5 | 15 | 15* | 2 | 7 | 8* |
| 4 | 3-2 | 14 | 22 | 22* | 15 | 25 | 25* | 19 | 29 | 20* | 17 | 25 | 26* | 12 | 19 | 20* |
| 5 | 4 | 18 | 27 | 30* | 15 | 23 | 24* | 12 | 20 | 20* | 11 | 18 | 19* | 15 | 24 | 24* |
| 6 | 3-1 | 6 | 16 | 15 | 8 | 19 | 21* | 3 | 18 | 18* | 5 | 11 | 15* | 5 | 14 | 15* |
| 7 | Pp | 2 | 6 | 5 | 7 | 11 | 11* | 1 | 7 | 8* | 8 | 12 | 13* | 1 | 6 | 6* |

P - practice test          C - contract          F - final test score          * - Bonus

Appendix B shows the records of seven children for a five-week period. The child's reading level is indicated and his pretest (P) score, his contract (C) which includes his pretest words plus new words, and his final (F) test score. Note the successes (*) of all children when paced appropriately.

## Appendix C

*Children's opinions of project.* Reactions are the written comments of the third grade children involved in the project described in this paper.

1. Spelling

   I like making my own spelling list because it is fun thinking up words.
   It is fun and the teacher does not have to work as much.
   I like to make the spelling list because you can study the words you put on the chart. I like to pick my own words to learn because I can pick words that are not too hard.
   You don't have to study the same words all the time. You have a selection.
   You can pick the easy words.
   I like picking my words because I don't get the word wrong that I wrote.
   I like making my own list because I learn what I want to. I don't have to do all the words.
   If I want to learn a word, all I have to do is put it on the list.
   You can pick words that you think will help. I like making my own spelling list because when the teacher does it, she has such easy words.
   I like picking my words because you can pick one word and learn nineteen and get a good letter. I like the idea because we can learn new words that we don't know how to spell. I like to see how many words I can think of to put on the list.
   Some people put some words that are too hard on the chart.

2. Open Groups

   I like open groups because you can read a different kind of story.
   I like the open reading groups because I get to read with different people.
   Sometimes there are too many people. I like open groups because I can pick where I want to come to read. I like open groups because it is fun to listen to other stories. I like open reading groups because I like reading about two different things.
   Sometimes it takes too much time.
   The other groups might have a good story.
   I like to see if other people enjoy the story that we read.

3. Celebrity of the Week

   I like the celebrity because some day I might have my picture on the wall.

I like the celebrity because I like to get the nice cards.

I like it because I was a celebrity.

I like it because people write about me.

It's nice writing letters.

I like to have a celebrity of the week because I can find things about people.

You can find if people like you.

When it comes my turn to be the celebrity, I can see what kind of good things there are about me.

I like it because the person gets a chance to be good.

If you're new, you get to know everybody.

I like the celebrity of the week because you don't need a stamp.

It makes me feel good when somebody writes something nice about me.

4. Self-evaluation

I think it is helpful. It does no harm.

I write my opinions on my paper because then I know what my grades would probably be.

It helps me learn.

I think we should check our own papers so you will know what our opinions are.

I think it is a good idea for us to check our work because we can show what we think about our papers.

It's hard for me to tell if five wrong is satisfactory.

I think its a good idea because right away we know how many we got right.

I like to check my work because after that I will know if I need to improve it or not. I would also know the grade I should get on my report card.

I like self-evaluation because you can find out the thing you do not know so that you can learn it.

I think self-evaluation is a good idea. I did not do this in second or first grade so I sometimes have trouble, but I like to do it.

# THE NEW SECONDARY READING TEACHER: PROBLEMS AND CONCERNS

*Wallace Z. Ramsey*
*University of Missouri at St. Louis*

"It's hard to avoid reading because every wheres we go reading is there," observed one secondary school student in Bel Kaufman's *Up the Down Stair Case.* The need to read in order to get along in secondary school is underscored by teachers in nearly all subjects. A concomitant need for almost every teacher to know how to teach students to read and use reading in their study, however, is frequently not realized by teachers until actual classroom teaching begins.

Many programs of secondary teacher education are so exclusively content oriented, with the how-to-do-it segment stripped to the bare bones, that the kinds of experience which reveal the nature of the real world of teaching are omitted. Courses in how to teach reading, or help students use reading in their study, are frequently available— but only on an elective basis. The requirements of general education and the areas of concentration in teaching fields are so stringent that little time remains for any kind of elective. The press of numbers and the nature of the professional education segment frequently deprive the neophyte of the realization of his own weaknesses in meeting the reading needs of his future students.

The content and procedures actually used in secondary reading methods courses are not too well known since the area has not been extensively researched. The problems faced by secondary teachers in reading and their perceptions of them are similar areas lacking information. The extent to which secondary teachers are actually trained in reading and their impressions concerning the value of certain aspects of their training are also not very well known.

A 136-item questionnaire designed to reveal the problems and concerns of secondary teachers in relation to teaching reading and using reading was completed by 308 teachers representing various geographical areas and types of schools. Over 95 percent of the teachers were in their first year of teaching.

### Responses from Reading Teachers

The teachers in the study were not well educated in reading. That only one-half had taken even one course in teaching reading and only one-sixth had completed a course in diagnostic and remedial reading may explain the nature of many responses.

The 61 reading teachers in the sample (most of whom also taught English) felt the greatest confidence in teaching the skills related to phonics, dictionary use, and word meanings (from 56 percent to 90 percent felt they were "adequate" to "very adequate" in these areas) and in the ability to use supplementary reading materials. They felt the least confident in constructing appropriate tests, in diagnosing reading problems, and in remedying reading problems (fewer than one-third felt adequate or very adequate in these areas). The general appraisal of their adequacy in teaching reading was not outstanding—in only four of the twenty-five tasks in teaching reading did a majority of the teachers rate themselves as adequate or very adequate.

The reading teachers were asked to evaluate those aspects of the college program which prepared them for teaching reading (this appraisal, of course, was to include more than methods courses). Of the teaching procedures used in the courses, those rated as "very helpful" or "helpful" a large portion of the time were demonstrations, classroom observation of reading instruction, and tutoring a child. Procedures rated low in value were lectures and uses of films, records, and audiotapes. Simulation, microteaching, and the use of television were reported as being "not used" in the classes taken by over one-half of the respondents.

When asked to rate the value of the various inservice aids in teaching reading that were provided by their school systems or were available in their area, over 80 percent of the teachers indicated that college or university courses in teaching reading were of "greatest value." Observing master teachers and consulting with a reading coordinator were also rated fairly high in value. Reading teachers were unenthusiastic about the value of consulting with their principals, using the professional library, and participating in interschool visitation. Over 60 percent reported that attendance at local, state, or national IRA meetings was "not available" to them.

### Content Teacher Responses

Less than 12 percent of the 250 content area teachers sampled had received any training in teaching reading, even as a small part of a larger course in general methods or special methods. Each respondent checked the proportion of his students having significant problems in reading material for class. Most responses ranged between 25 percent and 50 percent, with a mean of 38 percent.

A checklist of specific difficulties revealed that "understanding what they read" was cited most often as a problem, with "reading critically" and "knowing the meanings of words" rated closely behind. All three were checked as being difficult "frequently" or "very frequently" by over 70 percent of the respondents.

The two areas most commonly checked as "rarely" or "very rarely" existing as difficulties were "using the dictionary" and "discussing what they have read" (the latter probably being interpreted to mean "talking about what they have read"). Areas in which there was less consistency of agreement were "recognizing the words," "reading rapidly enough," "concentrating," "locating helpful reading material," and "remembering what they have read."

Respondents felt greatest confidence in ability to "teach key vocabulary," "ask stimulating questions to guide discussion," and "make assignments." They reported the greatest amount of difficulty in improving speed and in individualizing instruction.

Twelve potentially valuable partial solutions to the reading problems were listed, and respondents were asked to check each solution for desirability and practicality. The top-rated measure in the two categories combined was "training content teachers to teach reading skills." High on the list of desirable practices were remedial reading for poor readers, the use of multilevel textbooks, and a greater use of audiovisual aids in teaching. Rejected as undesirable were "retention of poor readers until they can read up to grade level" and "more extensive use of the lecture."

The responses concerning the value of inservice helps were similar to those of the reading teachers in the sample. The value of college and university courses was underscored by most.

When asked to list other problems encountered in helping their students use reading, responses were quite varied. An illustrative sample of remarks follows:

Not enough freedom to choose materials which fit students' needs.
Classes too large for individual help.
Not enough knowledge of what created reading problems and how to cope with the sources of these problems.
Student's inability to see relevance of reading to daily existence.

A second open-ended question asked respondents to pose additional solutions to the problems students encounter in using reading as a means of learning. Sample solutions included the following:

More background education for myself.

More effort on my part to try to meet individual needs and problems of students.

Greater effort to obtain materials suitable for each student.

Perhaps reading materials that relate to student problems concerning life and family and friends.

Besides gearing the reading material to student level of comprehension, much could be done to improve the reading material content in various subject areas.

Reading programs in every school which include not only remedial reading but how to read, take notes, evaluate importance, etc.

Greater use of many sources of reading materials.

Multilevel material, more laboratory exercises, independent work.

## Discussion of Findings

The low level of training in teaching reading by teachers in this study is contrary to most recommendations and may help to explain the lack of greater scholastic success in secondary education.

The use of a wide variety of techniques by professors in teacher education reading methods courses is certainly deserving of praise, but the lack of the value of such techniques, as indicated by respondents' low ratings, suggests the need for improvement of the quality of the techniques used. In other words, better demonstrations, better observations, better audio and videotapes, better films and filmstrips, and better lectures are all important needs in reading methods courses. At the same time an increase in the number of programs utilizing clinical observation, microteaching, and tutoring of children is clearly in order.

The finding that 40 percent of reading teachers rated themselves as adequate or above in all ratings is indicative of some general success of reading training programs (depending, of course, on the criterion level equated with *success*), but the problems pinpointed by respondents (such as weaknesses in constructing tests, information about new developments in reading, and poor ability to do diagnostic and remedial teaching) point the way to topics needing a more extensive treatment in training programs.

The self-ratings of the respondents may or may not be indicative for their actual skill in carrying out the various tasks in teaching reading. There is a need for studies which compare self-ratings with those made by university personnel or school supervisory personnel. Then one could say with much more confidence whether teachers are accurate in appraising their own strengths, weaknesses, and needs.

The findings in this study which are related to inservice helps have implications for both teacher education systems and school systems employing reading teachers. Since 80 percent of inservice teachers replied that college or university attendance was of the greatest value to them, teacher training institutions ought to continue to provide opportunities for inservice education for reading teachers through course offerings and to continue to improve upon those offerings where they are thin.

School systems, if they are to implement the findings from this study, will provide increased opportunities for interschool visitation, more reading workshops, better curriculum guides in reading, better reading committee functions, improved professional libraries, and more opportunities to observe master teachers of reading.

The best summary statement that can be made about the responses of content area teachers to the questionnaire is that teachers believe that 1) far too few have had training in reading, 2) a high proportion of their students have significant problems in reading material for class, 3) they have a general lack of knowledge concerning what to do about their students' reading problems, and 4) they have far too little effective help in coping with problems. Almost no agency can take pride in what has been done to aid content area teachers in helping their students to effectively use reading as a means of learning. There is a need for reform in both the quantity and quality of effort.

Colleges and universities should work to require future content area secondary teachers to be trained in reading or else to make elective courses for students so helpful that students will flock to the courses. The latter would probably be a wiser course.

School systems need to provide much more opportunity for content teachers to become oriented to the reading problems of students and to the methods and materials used in adjusting to the problems.

The International Reading Association should endeavor to make more national conventions, state IRA meetings, and local IRA programs (especially those related to secondary reading) available to secondary teachers. One cardinal need that the writer has observed is for local and district IRA meetings to be more problem-oriented. There is an excessive tendency to utilize "spellbinders" from the national IRA speakers' circuit. The need for help is simply not being met, and the combined efforts of all interested and knowledgeable persons are demanded to solve the problem.

The solutions to the content area reading problem which were supported by teachers in the study generally are those supported by reading specialists. There is no basic philosophical disagreement over what should be done. The emotional climate for effective action is good; cooperative effort is what is needed. College and university personnel should respond to this opportunity.

# CONTINUING PROFESSIONAL EXPERIENCES
# IN READING

*John C. Manning*
*University of Minnesota*

There appears to be general agreement among reading educators that neither the number nor the quality of undergraduate reading methods preparation is sufficient to meet the demands of teaching all the children of all the citizens to read.

Criticism of teacher education programs in reading and other elementary subject matter areas has been chronic. Some criticism, notably Austin's *The First R*, has been scholarly and significant. Most criticism, however, has been subjective, emotional, and evasive. Indeed, criticizing teacher education programs may well be the last public enjoyment of the academician.

Impelled by the vogue of behavioral objectives, a considerable number of undergraduate teacher education models have been generated for discussion and hopeful use. I trust that we have really effective people for the proposed effective models.

The continuing professional experiences or inservice scene is another matter entirely. Degrees of criticism of inservice efforts may range from none at all, since no inservice experiences are available, to severe criticism since too many experiences of the wrong kind are available and even at times are required.

There are at least three dimensions to the continuing professional experiences situation: 1) formal course work of the extension variety usually directed toward suburban or rural area reading problems, 2) formal course work at colleges or universities, and 3) inservice activities conducted in public school settings during the school year or in the summer months.

Perhaps I'm creating a false dichotomy but I should like to define formal course work in university settings as professional or theoretical preparation. Extension course experiences and other public school conducted activities I would define as technical preparation. Both types of preparation are obviously necessary for the effective teacher of reading, but I submit that the main problems which plague the reading practitioners are much more technical than professional. And I might add that we are all practitioners, or we should be. This discussion presents in modest detail those continuing experiences that are technical or public school oriented in nature.

To be effective, extension type courses should combine preparatory lecture/discussion and classroom practice activities. Such combined activity courses offer the greatest possibilities for changing teacher behavior and improving the quality of reading instruction.

The student populations for such courses should be limited to single school districts of a small size or to primary grade teachers or first grade teachers or to other personnel units which reduce the range of possible course content in a realistic manner. Many extension type courses are meaningless because they attempt to do all things for all teachers.

The course content of extension type continuing experiences should be organized to provide practitioners access to basal, ancillary, and enrichment reading materials available and appropriate for the classroom populations. Further, the course should include discussions of instructional techniques which have been effective in teaching children to read. Much inservice participation is evasive and irrelevant since it avoids the realities of existing reading materials and the standard practices of participating classroom teachers.

The activities described to this point could very well be conducted in the late afternoon or evening though I am unalterably committed to the goal that all inservice activities be conducted during the regular school day with released time provided to teachers and alternative programs developed for pupils affected by the inservice activites.

The late afternoon or evening discussions of extension type inservice activities should be followed by at least a full day of purposeful supervisory activities by the course instructor. Quite simply, the course instructor should visit the classrooms of his teacher-students to determine his own instructional significance. During classroom visits the course instructor should use demonstration teaching as a major vehicle for changing classroom behaviors. Further, involvement in the daily school reading program increases the likelihood that lectures and discussions will be germane to existing classroom conditions and problems. In summary, extension type activities should 1) combine discussion and practice, 2) serve a realistic grade range of involved practitioners, 3) be specific and relevant to existing instructional conditions, and 4) involve supervision of classroom practice by the course instructor.

The possibilities are extensive for a variety of inservice activities in public school settings during the regular school year and during the summer. After school meetings, Saturday conferences, professional conferences, minimum day, and limited day meetings are regularly conducted in most school districts during the school year. Indeed, as we seem to polarize on a labor management axis, such continuing inservice activities are quite prominent in the negotiation proceedings. Such incidental and sporadic meetings, while well intended, do not in my judgment produce meaningful results. The discussion here will focus on two types of public school inservice activities: presummer school experiences and major inservice summer and school year programs.

Summer school reading programs can provide rich educational opportunities for children and a lively laboratory for teachers equipped with newly-learned instructional skills. An inservice program for teachers should be conducted prior to the actual summer school program.

This paper focuses on the five-day preparation programs which are conducted for all teachers in the Minneapolis Public Schools' summer programs.

Teachers of children entering kindergarten in September receive instruction on classroom procedures for an effective six weeks prekindergarten summer school experience. This inservice training program stresses theories and practices related to oral language development for innercity preschool children. The morning hours are devoted to instructional practices and procedures, while in the afternoon sessions teachers assemble and organize the instructional materials.

In separate sessions, teachers who will teach children entering first grade also receive instruction with methods and materials essential to an effective prefirst summer school program. This prefirst program stresses language development, letter recognition, sound symbol correspondence skills, and written language experience activities. Teachers who teach children at other grade levels receive instruction in classroom procedures related to a summer reading program written specifically for Minneapolis Public School children.

These summer inservice efforts are characterized by demonstration teaching with the provision of relevant instructional material for classroom use. These two provisions to my mind affect teacher instructional behaviors more significantly than any other inservice variables.

Space does not allow a detailed explanation of the major in-service teacher education program in reading being conducted currently in the Minneapolis Public Schools. The Combine Project is a comprehensive and combined effort to resolve the reading problems of innercity children. Personnel from the North and South-Central Pyramid complexes of the public schools, undergraduate and graduate students of the University of Minnesota, and university teachers are involved in this massive and significant effort. Two Combine Centers have been established, one at the Hawthorne School in the North Pyramid and one at the Lyndale School in the South. Five hundred educationally disadvantaged children in the two centers are given additional instruction in reading to augment that of the classroom teacher. Planned, supervised, and systematic individual tutoring and small group instruction is provided by juniors and seniors of the University of Minnesota who are enrolled in two reading methods course sections. Ten reading specialist interns supervise the activities of the undergraduates. These interns are full time masters candidates who supervise the teaching experiences of the undergraduates and who are assigned ultimately as resource teachers to elementary schools in the innercity. Twenty such reading specialists have been trained, one for each of the elementary schools of the Pyramids.

Two clinically trained doctoral candidates teach the undergraduate reading methods courses and assist with supervision of the undergraduates. Two primary reading specialists and two intermediate specialists are assigned to the Pyramid Reading Task Force.

The inservice aspects of the Combine Project involve continuous inservice programs for teachers at all levels during the school year and in the summer months. The Combine Project is supported logistically by an instructional materials center and a writing team capable of producing, printing, and distributing instructional materials for children on telephoned request of classroom teachers. In most instances, developed and printed materials for children are available on the morning following the request.

# A MAXIMUM INPUT
# JUNIOR HIGH SCHOOL WORKSHOP

*Emmaline Henriksen*
*and*
*Carl Rosen*
*Kent State University*

As a part of a national survey in 1963, Austin and Morrison (*1*) concluded that inservice programs for reading should be designed to 1) involve the classroom teachers in planning the content of the program, 2) provide for released class time for participation, 3) utilize a variety of audiovisual techniques and materials, 4) allow for active participation of the teachers, and 5) include the participation of administrative officials concerned with guidance of teachers in inservice activities for the improvement of personnel within the system.

Other studies seem to repeat these recommendations with special emphasis upon the content of the workshop centering on the special concerns or problems that teachers possess in regard to their given grade level or content area. Moburg (*2*) reviewed the research (1963-1972) dealing with inservice programs in reading and found that most of the studies reported on projects for elementary teachers. He cited only three projects involving the secondary teacher. Reading specialists conducting such workshops frequently impose expectations of resistance by secondary teachers to reading and elementary school orientations to the conceptualization of an inservice program for secondary level teachers. Frequently, the results are as expected. This paper describes a workshop for junior high school level teachers which was designed to deal with this issue as well as those points described in Austin and Morrison's book.

Because the range of reading abilities tends to spread as individuals grow older, it would not be unnatural to find that the range of abilities in a typical seventh grade class might include reading grade levels from 2.5 to 9.5. Thus, teachers at the junior high school level must be prepared to provide differentiated instruction in all areas of the curriculum. Such situations call for high level understanding of not only one's subject and textbooks but also an understanding of methods for studying and determining the reading abilities of students, a grasp of the reading processes, and knowledge of diversified techniques for teaching one's subject and organizing a class based upon individual differences in reading.

Due to the nature of college preparatory programs for junior and senior high school teachers, many content area teachers have little or no knowledge of the reading process, methods, strategies and/or materials used in the teaching of reading. Because research has shown that the teacher is a critical factor in the success or failure of a program and, by nature of the fact that the reading skills and abilities needed in a content area are vital, it appears that the content area teacher is in the key position for developing the needed reading skills simultaneously within the content of a given area. Workshops seem to represent a key approach towards developing such skills, concepts, and abilities.

## The Workshop

Because school districts frequently require participation in in-service workshops, usually there is an initial lack of interest and negative attitude, thus placing a heavy burden on the workshop staff to improve such conditions. This situation was not atypical of the workshop to be described in this paper. This workshop was designed to develop interests, attitudes, knowledge, skills, and abilities which would enhance the teacher's potential to improve reading and, hence, learning in the subject matter fields.

With these goals in mind, the staff identified and defined specific areas of concern at the junior high school level. In-depth planning included consideration of the best techniques for presentation and involvement of the participants.

Before the outline of topics to be covered in the workshop was presented to the participants, the group was divided into small sections to discuss immediate needs and concerns. The small group discussions included questions similar to the ones which follow as guidelines:

1. What responsibilities do you feel you have to students who are not succeeding in your classroom?
2. What did your college or university emphasize in preparing you for teaching? Content, method, or both?
3. How much time do you spend in considering teaching techniques and the selection of diversified reading matter as compared to preparing for introduction of content and textbook work?

4. How do you react when discussions involve such topics as reading instruction, poor readers, report card grades, discipline, elementary schools' responsibilities for reading instruction, and failing children in elementary schools?

It was found from these discussion sessions that the projected areas to be presented in the workshop included specific participant needs and interests.

## Content

The content of the workshop was as follows:

1. *Fundamental Issues in Reading in Secondary Schools*
   Place of reading in school and society, development of reading during school years, nature of differences in reading among secondary pupils, reading and the role of secondary schools.

2. *Nature of Reading Process and Some Linguistic Premises*
   Reading as a phase of the communication process with emphasis on classroom application in secondary schools, influence of linguistic factors on reading, the role of spoken and written language behavior, issues pertaining to dialect, and psycholinguistics as applied to reading content areas in secondary schools.

3. *Overview of Fundamental Skills and Abilities in Reading*
   Word recognition, comprehension, reading interests and attitudes, comprehension in the content areas.

4. *Evaluation of Reading by Classroom Teachers in Secondary Schools*
   Classroom and group techniques for evaluation of reading for purposes of determining range of reading within a class, individual pupil level of general reading ability, modified reading diagnostic procedures for individual pupil assessment, assessing readability of texts and instructional materials, and the implications of readability on instructional procedures.

5. *Teaching Techniques for Dealing with Individual Differences in Reading*
   Matching and adjusting difficulty level of content materials (readability) to pupils' reading abilities, grouping arrangements, choosing content, diversification of materials, new media approaches, differentiation of expectations, techniques of teaching a selection.

## Staff

The staff of the workshop consisted of seven persons with diversified training and experience in the field of reading and in teaching (two university professors and five graduate students in reading with a range of teaching experience in the public schools from first grade through secondary level). In addition to the regular staff, two consultants were brought in from other universities to work with the participants on differentiation of instruction and student involvement.

## Participants

The participants of the workshop were from two innercity junior high schools and included 75 teachers representing all curriculum areas, 3 reading teachers, 8 paraprofessionals, 4 parents, and 8 administrative personnel for a total of 98 participants. A questionnaire revealed that none of the participants, with the exception of the reading specialists, had had any courses in reading or experience in the teaching of reading.

## Schedule

The workshop consisted of twelve four-hour sessions which met Monday through Thursday evenings for three consecutive weeks. Each four-hour session was divided into two periods with a thirty minute break between sessions. The first session included the total group of participants and was exploratory in nature. The topics presented involved active participation of the group when feasible. Following the break, the participants were organized into small groups according to content areas, interests, and/or topics. Each small group was conducted by two staff members, and the topic explored in the large group session was further developed as it related to the interests of each group.

## Techniques

A variety of techniques was used in an effort to maximize participant involvement, stimulate interest, and develop a better understanding of reading and its relationship to the junior high level content areas. The following examples are indicative of the diversified techniques employed:

1. Pre- and postassessment of teacher opinions related to the teaching of reading.
2. Pre- and postassessment involving a self-evaluation form of reading concepts based on the four basic goals of the workshop.

3. Presentation and discussion of three case studies of junior high school students to enable participants to gain insights into both "Why a Workshop in Reading?" and the nature of individual differences in reading among junior high school students.

4. Participation in a learning to read experience involving a primer, *Mr. Geography,* which utilized symbols other than the traditional orthography thus enabling participants to experience the kinds of difficulties encountered by beginners in both the learning to read process and the failure to read process.

5. Tape recordings of dialect were used in small group sessions in an effort to foster further understanding of the relationship of dialect, language, and reading.

6. Specific word recognition activities were designed to include active involvement of participants in unlocking unknown words. Participants then developed specific activities within their content area for expanding individual word attack skills.

7. An activity requiring participants to assign difficulty levels to various comprehension tasks was presented. The purpose was to develop teaching skills that would enhance student interest and involvement as well as to refine understanding of the comprehension abilities.

8. The latter activity led to application of the concept of three levels of comprehension (literal, interpretative, and critical) within the content areas. Participants then used magazines, textbooks, and a variety of other materials to develop comprehension activities for differentiated instruction within their classrooms.

9. Literary and scientific passages with comprehension checks were used within a given time limit to enable subjects to further develop an understanding of differentiated rate of reading along with comprehension.

10. A readability formula was introduced and discussed by means of an active involvement technique in which the teachers determined the readability of their own materials.

11. Creative teaching techniques were generated from idea-sharing sessions in small groups. These techniques were primarily for motivating student involvement utilizing unit approaches for instruction.

12. A group informal reading inventory was administered to participants divided according to content areas. The test

was designed from the students' own textbooks. The scoring and interpretation of results were demonstrated via participants' own performance. Emphasis was placed on determining instructional levels and minimal individual diagnosis for rate of reading and comprehension.

13. Profiles and characteristics of below average, average, and advanced readers were examined. Participants categorized specific activities for differentiating instruction for the three groups of readers. Exercises for differentiating instruction were then developed within the content areas.

## Materials

In addition to the textbook (3), various other materials were used to develop the overall objectives—case studies, transparencies, tapes, a film on the handicapped reader, magazines, newspapers, content area textbooks, and teacher-made materials.

## Evaluation

A pre- and postassessment of the participants involved the completion of two questionnaires. One of the forms was a self-evaluation form of twenty-five reading concepts keyed to four major topics. Each participant was instructed to respond to each concept on the basis of both knowledge of and ability to apply the concept in his current school position. The rating scale categories were *Don't Know, Don't Use; Know, But Don't Use;* and *Know and Use.* Table 1 presents the pre- and post-workshop assessment for concept mastery.

A study of Table 1 shows that the greater majority of the workshop participants in the pretest phase rated their understanding and use of major concepts in the *Don't Know, Don't Use* category. This was significantly reversed in the posttest phase in favor of the *Know and Use* category. These data demonstrate the heavy influence

**TABLE 1**

Pre- and Postassessment of Concept Mastery
Based on Four Major Topics for a Junior
High School Workshop in Reading

| MAJOR TOPICS | % of Responses From Pre- and Postassessment | | | | | | | |
| --- | --- | --- | --- | --- | --- | --- | --- | --- |
| | Don't Know Don't Use | | Know Don't Use | | Know-Use | | No Response | |
| | Pre | Post | Pre | Post | Pre | Post | Pre | Post |
| Diagnosis of Abilities | 64% | 7% | 17% | 23% | 12% | 66% | 7% | 4% |
| Reading Process | 56% | 8% | 14% | 22% | 25% | 67% | 5% | 4% |
| Diversified Techniques | 62% | 6% | 11% | 19% | 20% | 73% | 7% | 2% |
| Differentiated Instruction | 47% | 7% | 16% | 20% | 31% | 69% | 6% | 4% |

of the workshop in learning concepts and in fostering intentions to use these in future classroom work.

The second phase of the pre- and postassessment involved a questionnaire to survey opinions about reading practices. The questionnaire consisted of twenty-five items in which participants were to choose one of the following as a response to an item-statement within the framework of both practical and personal agreement or disagreement: *Disagree, No opinion,* and *Agree.*

The items on the inventory generally dealt with teacher attitudes toward four major topics of the workshop. As an example, one item dealing with *diagnosis* was, "Students' reading abilities should be known by teachers"; one item dealing with the *reading process* was, "Subject matter teachers should understand what reading skills and abilities are required for reading in their subject"; one item dealing with *diversified teaching techniques* was "Various plans for grouping should be utilized rather than be limited to continuous lecture style"; and, finally, an item dealing with *differentiated instruction* was, "Both assignments and tests should be differentiated for poor and good readers."

Table 2 presents the pre- and postassessment data based upon percent of responses in the various attitude categories by major workshop objectives. Attitudinal response percentage for individual items constituting the four major topics were totaled in pre- and post phases.

Responses to the survey provide evidence that positive values were present and only minimally modified in the plus direction at the end of the workshop. It is likely that these secondary teachers were unable to operationalize their attitudes due to a significant lack of knowledge of key concepts in reading and inability to apply them. Perhaps one major problem of reading specialists conducting workshops with secondary teachers might be the assumption that these professionals are far more negative than they actually are.

TABLE 2

Pre- and Postassessment of Opinions
Referring to Four Major Topics for
a Junior High School Workshop in Reading

| MAJOR TOPICS | % Responses From Pre- and Postassessment | | | | | | | |
| | Disagree | | No Opinion | | Agree | | No Response | |
| | Pre | Post | Pre | Post | Pre | Post | Pre | Post |
|---|---|---|---|---|---|---|---|---|
| Diagnosis of Abilities | 3% | 0% | 15% | 4% | 80% | 94% | 2% | 2% |
| Reading Process | 4% | 3% | 12% | 7% | 83% | 88% | 1% | 2% |
| Diversified Techniques | 2% | 1% | 11% | 4% | 86% | 93% | 1% | 1% |
| Differentiated Instruction | 7% | 2% | 10% | 5% | 81% | 92% | 2% | 1% |

A general questionnaire revealed that, upon completion of the workshop, approximately 50 percent of the participants indicated an intent to take further courses in reading and 53 percent felt a high degree of responsibility for the teaching of reading in their given situation. The influence of the workshop on these intentions can only be assumed.

## Conclusion

One of the more significant conclusions from this workshop is that maximum input and active participation of both participants and staff provide for a highly successful learning situation. The staff and participants were thoroughly changed professionals from this experience. Cooperative planning, sharing responsibilities, daily troubleshooting, flexible planning, and creative teaching provided a model for the participants as well as for the staff.

The pre- and posttest data showed significant gains in concept mastery and in intention to apply in classroom work. The findings reference to the participants' general pre-workshop attitudes highlights the "ripeness" for such workshops. A follow up between the staff and participants is scheduled for the coming year.

**References**

1. Austin, Mary C., and Coleman Morrison. *The First R: The Harvard Report on Reading in Elementary School.* New York: Macmillan, 1963.

2. Moburg, Lawrence G. *Inservice Teacher Training in Reading.* Newark, Delaware: International Reading Association, 1972.

3. Olson, A., and W. Ames. (Eds.). *Teaching Reading Skills in Secondary Schools: Readings.* Scranton, Pennsylvania: International Textbook, 1970.

# TAKING BELLYACHING OUT OF MODULE MAKING

*Lee H. Mountain*
*University of Houston*

Recently, educators have become "bewitched, bothered, and be-wildered" by the competency based movement with its instructional modules. The claims for competency based programs are certainly bewitching. The modular approach is supposed to help teachers become as competent in the classroom as obstetricians are in the delivery room. That's a bewitching prospect. But many an educator has become bothered and bewildered while trying to move toward that prospect.

Much of the bother and bewilderment is generated by the favor-ite instructional vehicle of the competency based movement—*the module.* A module is an instructional package that leads to compe-tency. It has some characteristics in common with a map. It points out the learner's destination (objective) and some good routes for getting there (learning activities). It also gives the student landmarks for judging whether he has arrived (pretest and posttest).

Well-designed modules give structure and substance to a compe-tency based program. Upon completion of the modules leading to certification as a reading teacher, a candidate would be able to demonstrate these competencies:

| | |
|---|---|
| He knows his subject, reading. | (Knowledge) |
| He can teach reading. | (Performance) |
| His pupils learn to read. | (Results) |

It isn't easy to design modules that establish a student's compe-tencies in the areas of knowledge, performance, and results. But many education professors are making valiant attempts to design such modules. In about half of our states, education courses are being restructured to fit competency based programs. Consequently, many man-hours are going into module making.

## The Need for Simplicity

Perhaps some of those hours could be saved if module makers could start with a short, simple format in hand. Much of the bellyaching associated with module making happens right at the onset of the job when the module maker tries to arrive at a format. Various formats include all of the following elements:

| | | |
|---|---|---|
| Prospectus | Preassessment | Criterion behaviors |
| Introduction | Overview | Learning experiences |
| Rationale | Instructional alternatives | Evaluation |
| Objectives | Flow chart | Recycles |
| Prerequisites | Professional entry level | Postassessment |
| Competencies | Enablers | Conclusion |

This listing is the type of thing that inspired Mason (4) to satirize modules. Obviously, any module that included all eighteen of the preceding elements would be too cumbersome for practical use. Sartain and Stanton (5), Howsam (3), Houston (2), and Arends (1) have suggested module formats that contain the essentials within five to seven parts. They, along with other proponents of competency based education, stress the desirability of streamlining module format.

## Format and Wording

The three parts that appear with greatest regularity in modules are the 1) objective, 2) learning activities, and 3) assessments (pretest and posttest). These three parts seem to be the musts of a module. The objective can't be eliminated since it names the goal and thereby determines the content. The pretest and posttest can't be eliminated since they determine whether or not the goal has been reached. The learning activities certainly can't be eliminated since they enable the student to establish his competencies in the areas of knowledge, performance, and/or results. So the simplest possible format for a module has to include the objective, pretest and posttest, and learning activities.

Simplifying the format, however, is only the first step in taking the bellyaching out of module making. This module skeleton must be fleshed out with sentences and paragraphs. The module maker faces the formidable task of wording his thoughts to fit the format. It is always difficult to communicate by putting sentences on paper. But it is doubly difficult when the words *objective, pretest, posttest,* and *learning activities* must leap out meaningfully from the material.

One frustrated module writer commented, "I wish the competency based experts would take a lesson from bill collection agencies. Those agencies have developed standard wordings for their letters.

The first letter uses very polite language to tell you your bill is overdue. Then the wording in each succeeding letter gets stronger. But the agent doesn't have to waste his time composing these letters. All he has to do is fill in the blanks with your name and the amount you owe. I wish the competency based experts would work out some standard wording and give me a fill-in-the-blanks form for a module starter."

If our society can produce fill-in-the-blanks forms for everything from recommendations to love letters, perhaps the idea of a fill-in-the-blanks module starter isn't too farfetched. It would be no more than an expanded outline. It could serve only as the roughest of rough drafts. Still it might save module makers a little time at the onset of the job. It might provide wording for a few of the opening sentences that are so hard to get down on paper.

### The Module Starter

So, in the interest of hastening progress toward competency based teacher education, I worked out the Module Starter which follows. You can fill in the blanks with almost any topic. You can use the standard wording of the opening paragraphs to show that your format includes an objective, pretest and posttest, and learning activities. You can, in effect, sprint for the first 100 yards of your cross-country run in module making.

The Module Starter, however, carries you over only the first 100 yards. For the rest of the module making job, you are running on your own power.

Later in this article you will see how the Module Starter can be used to speed up the production of a working draft. You also will see what a working draft looks like, after it has been derived from the Module Starter shown.

### MODULE STARTER

Topic: _____

*Objective:* After the learning activities on _____, you will be able to answer yes to each question below, and back up each yes with the required performance.

Ask yourself these questions now as your *pretest.* Use them again as your *posttest* when you finish the module. The sentences after each question will give you an overview of the *learning activities* in this module.

KNOWLEDGE QUESTION(S)

Can you expand your concept of _____? To find out, try Learning Activity #1. Your first step in this activity will be to write a paragraph on _____ that reflects your point of view right now. Your last step will be to write a paragraph on _____ that reflects your point of view upon completion of this module.

As you add other "knowledge" questions that deal with important parts of your module topic, you might use this wording:

Can you (name, list, match, identify, define, describe) _____? If not, try Learning Activity # ___. During this activity you will . . . .

PERFORMANCE QUESTION(S)

Can you design and teach a lesson on _____? For guidelines, see Learning Activity # ___. In this activity you will _____ (tape record or videotape your presentation, interview people about your topic and present information to them informally, roleplay your lesson with peers, work with a class of children).

RESULTS QUESTION(S)

Can you give evidence that your pupil(s) learned what you taught about _____? For guidelines see Learning Activity # ___. During this activity you will _____ (write a notebook report on what your pupils did, submit children's tests and scores, do a self evaluation by checksheet, get a peer evaluation by rating scale).

## A Way to Save Time

The following conversation shows how two professors approached the Module Starter. One thought it could save him some time, so he wanted to use it. The other was reluctant, but he finally agreed to give it a try.

You will see that they settled for just filling in the blanks *only* at the very beginning of their module making. Soon they started changing the wording, expanding some parts, deleting others, and adapting the material to fit their topic and their program. This is the way the Starter should be used. It is a launching pad, not a mold.

The opening page of the module finally produced by these two professors adheres fairly closely to the format of the Module Starter. However, the professors changed the wording in many places, and they added material on their particular topic. The Starter served mainly as a taking-off point for the two professors whose conversation is transcribed here:

He   We've been assigned to team teach the reading methods course in the competency based program. So we'll be writing modules together. Where do you want to start?

She   I don't want to start at all. I have a terrible time getting started on a module. It takes forever! By the time I've struggled through an introduction and a rationale and a list of prerequisites, I have writer's cramp.

He   Why be bothered with all those parts? Let's try the Module Starter for a

|       | shortcut. It might help us get a format and a few sentences on paper in a hurry. |
|-------|---|
| She   | Oh, no! None of that quick and dirty stuff for me. I'm a Ph.D., not a grade school dropout. I don't need a simplified format and standard wording. I'm scholarly. |
| He    | Well, I'm rushed. So let's see if the Module Starter can save us some writing time. |
| She   | Have it your way. But it won't work. There's no way to get off to a fast start on a module. |
| He    | We'll see. What's the first thing you want our students to be able to do in this reading methods course? What's your first objective? |
| She   | To start with, I want them to be able to describe the reading process. |
| He    | Okay, let's fill in the blank in the objective with that topic, *the reading process.* |

> Objective: After the learning activities on *the reading process,* you will be able to answer yes to each question below and back up each yes with the required performance.

| She   | That's too simple. It doesn't sound scholarly. To meet that objective, all you have to do is answer yes to the pretest and posttest questions. |
|-------|---|
| He    | But you have to back up each answer with the required performance. We'll word the pretest and posttest questions very carefully. We'll fix it so that the students can't answer yes to those questions without establishing their competencies. |
| She   | Okay, I'll live with that objective for now. Let's move on to the pretest. |
| He    | If we fill in the blanks for the first "knowledge" question, this is what we'll have: |

> Can you expand your concept of *the reading process?* To find out, try Learning Activity #1. Your first step in this activity will be to write a paragraph on *the reading process* that reflects your point of view right now. Your last step will be to write a paragraph on *the reading process* that reflects your point of view upon completion of this module.

| She   | Let's change that wording a little. Let's say *write a description of* instead of *write a paragraph on.* |
|-------|---|
| He    | Good idea! The Module Starter says that we should add other knowledge questions. How can we word those questions to get at more than one description of reading? We want our students to view reading as a decoding process and as a visual process and as a thinking process. |
| She   | Let's handle those three points of view in three questions for our pretest and posttest. |
| He    | All right. I'll try to get them down on paper. (After a minute he hands over this draft.) |

*Teacher Training*

Can you describe how you decode words that are unfamiliar to you? If not, try Learning Activity 2, "Reading as a Decoding Process."

Can you describe how your eyes operate while you're reading? If not, try Learning Activity 3, "Reading as a Visual Process."

Can you describe how you recognize, comprehend, and interpret printed material? If not, try Learning Activity 4, "Reading as a Thinking Process."

She    Not bad. You work on a learning activity to go with each of those questions. I'll fill in the blank in the performance question and then start revising it . . . .

Within the hour these two professors completed the opening page of their module on the reading process (shown in text below). As you can see, they adapted the Module Starter to suit their topic. Their expanded opener is detailed enough to serve as an overview of the whole module, but it is still short enough to fit on one page.

Their opening page gives only one learning activity for each question. This approach is adequate for module makers who are trying to produce a working draft in a hurry. Alternate routes to each goal are certainly desirable, but they can be added later.

The type of page shown, derived from the Module Starter, is easy to produce and understand. After a student reads the sentences following the knowledge questions (1-4), the performance question (5), and the results question (6), he knows how he can fulfill the objectives of this module.

### MODULE STARTER

Topic: *The Reading Process*

*Objective*: After the learning activities on the reading process you will be able to answer yes to each question below and back up each yes with the required performance.

Ask yourself these questions now as your *pretest*. Use them again as your *posttest* when you finish the module. The sentences after each question will give you an overview of the *learning activities* in this module.

1.  Can you expand your concept of the reading process? To find out, try Learning Activity 1, "The Big Picture." Your first step in this activity will be to write a description of the reading process that reflects your point of view right now. Your last step will be to write a description of the reading process that reflects your point of view upon completion of this module.

2.  Can you describe how you decode words that are unfamiliar to you? If not, try Learning Activity 2, "Reading as a Decoding Process." During this activity you will try to read a paragraph with your book turned upside down. This decoding experience will help you rediscover so

many of the difficulties of beginning readers.

3. Can you describe how your eyes operate while you're reading? If not, try Learning Activity 3, "Reading as a Visual Process." During this activity you will watch the eye movements of a reader so that you can spot fixations, saccadic movements, and return sweeps.

4. Can you describe how you recognize, comprehend, and interpret printed material? If not, try Learning Activity 4, "Reading as a Thinking Process." During this experience you'll study an article about the nature of reading.

5. Can you explain the decoding, visual, and/or thinking aspects of the reading process to two adults and two children? For guidelines, see Learning Activity 5, "Interviews with Readers." During this activity you will teach each interviewee three ways to look at the reading process.

6. Can you give evidence that one of your interviewees retained what you said about the reading process? For guidelines, see Learning Activity 6, "The Proof of the Pudding." During this activity you will check back with one of your interviewees from Activity 5. If, after a lapse of a day or more, that person can describe two of the three points of view that you presented about reading, you can write up a report of successful results.

## The Module Maker's Theme Song

Now that you have seen 1) the Module Starter, 2) a conversation about its use, and 3) an opening page derived from it, you are in a good position to decide whether it can take any of the bellyaching out of module making. If it can, the bellyachers may change their tune—or at least their lyrics.

These lyrics, set to the tune of "Bewitched, Bothered and Bewildered," express the feelings of the ex-bellyachers who have become competency based converts:

> We're modularized
>     and we're self-paced.
> Each field experience is
>     performance based.
> We're not
>     bothered and bewildered
>         by competency.
>
> Do we assess?
>     Oh, yes, yes, yes.
> We preassess and postassess
>     and reassess.
> Bewitched
>     by our students' competencies
>         are we.

**References**

1. Arends, Robert L., John Masla, and Wilford Weber. *Handbook for the Development of Instructional Modules in Competency Based Teacher Education Programs.* Buffalo, New York: Center for the Study of Teaching, 1973.

2. Houston, Robert, Loye Y. Hollis, and Howard Jones. *Developing Instructional Modules.* Houston, Texas: University of Houston, 1972.

3. Howsam, Robert B., and Robert Houston. *Competency Based Teacher Education.* Chicago, Illinois: Science Research Associates, 1972.

4. Mason, George E. "M.O.D.U.L.E. for Sale," *Journal of Reading Behavior,* 5 (Winter 1972-1973), 71-73.

5. Sartain, Harry W., and Paul E. Stanton (Eds.). *Modular Preparation for Teaching Reading.* Newark, Delaware: International Reading Association, 1974.

# reading
# specialists:
## qualifications and techniques

"What shall I say if my parents ask me if you are
an average or below average teacher?"

# QUALIFICATIONS AND SELECTION
# OF READING CONSULTANTS

*Lou E. Burmeister*
*University of Texas at El Paso*

Reading consultants, *in toto*, normally work with classroom teachers, remedial reading teachers, other faculty members, the administration, and the community. Any one consultant or team of consultants, however, might work with just one or a few of these—and not all of them.

For example, in one school system, consultant services might be organized vertically. In this system one consultant might serve just remedial reading teachers; another, just language arts teachers; and another, just content area teachers. In another school system, consultant services might be organized horizontally. In this system, one consultant might serve just primary level teachers; another, middle grade teachers; and another, junior and senior high school teachers. Still other systems are organized both horizontally and vertically, having a remedial reading consultant for the primary grades, another for the middle grades, etc.

## Fragmentation

Possible fragmentation in terms of personnel which a consultant serves may lead the consultant to specialize in a specific area and to become competent in that area. On the other hand, fragmentation may lead to a narrow and restricted view of the reading program for individual students and for the total school system and, thus, to a reading program that lacks coordination and articulation.

Such has been the case, for example, when remedial reading consultants and teachers have been unaware of what has been or is concurrently going on in their students' regular reading and/or content area classes. And in these various classes, the programs which individual students used were conflicting and incompatible.

Such has been the case, too, when reading consultants and teachers in developmental reading classes have made provisions for the variety of reading achievement levels and approaches in reading classes, per se. But when the same students were studying science or math or social studies, they were all expected to use the same textbook and the same approach. Such inconsistencies should never occur.

## Cooperative Effort is Necessary

To avoid such inconsistencies and to develop a strong program, reading consultants who serve a specific school or school system must make a cooperative effort in 1) developing a philosophy of reading; 2) designing a coordinated schoolwide reading program from K-12 in reading classes, in content area classes, and in remedial reading; 3) implementing the philosophy and schoolwide program in terms of individual differences in the needs, abilities, interests, and aspirations of students or groups of students; 4) implementing the philosophy and schoolwide program in terms of the individual capabilities, talents, and interests of teachers or groups of teachers; and 5) recognizing the need for ongoing evaluation, innovation, and change when such change may be desirable because of less than adequate success with an individual or group of students and because of research findings or new program development.

## Philosophy of Reading

Consultants in a schoolwide system must formulate a well-defined philosophy of reading which they are able to communicate to the administration, faculty, students, and community. Additionally, consultants individually and collectively should possess an openness, a sense of empathy and flexibility, which enables them to consider, evaluate, and adopt ideas from those with whom they work. Such flexibility should enable them to spearhead a continuously evolving and changing program suitable to the growing needs and expanding aspirations of the students and the community, to the talents of the teachers with whom they work, and to the national and international body of continuously growing research and development (1,3,5,6,7,8,12,13).

The philosophy which the consultants accept will mold the goals of the complete reading program. Such a philosophy might include the following objectives, stated in terms of desirable student behavior:

1. Continuous growth in reading abilities, such as in work recognition; in gaining a clear idea of the literal and interpretative

meanings the author intends; in reacting to these meanings critically, judiciously; and in extending these meanings or judgments through synthesizing or blending them with other ideas.

2. Continuous growth in speed of comprehension and in study skills.

3. Continuous growth in broadening and enriching interests and in improving taste in reading materials and in reading for a variety of purposes or effects (11), such as the following: the instrumental effect (reading done to solve a practical problem such as to pass a test, make a speech, bake a cake, build a bookcase); the prestige effect (reading done to ameliorate the reader's personal feelings about himself or a situation); reinforcement or conversion effect (reading done to further clarify an attitude or feeling or to change an attitude or feeling); aesthetic effect (reading done to enrich the reader's sense of beauty, character, setting, or theme); and respite (reading done for a holiday, for escape).

4. Continuous growth in the ability to recognize and formulate purposes for reading in light of the reader's needs and/or interests and the dictates of the writing style of the author and content of the material. Such growth involves, also, the ability to read for various purposes, the ability to shift gears in terms of comprehension skills and rates, and the use of those skills which are appropriate to the reader himself and his background and interest.

5. Continuous growth in resourcefulness in locating appropriate reading materials.

## Schoolwide Reading Program

A first step in implementing a philosophy of reading is frequently viewed through formulation of a K-12 program in terms of scope and sequence. In this respect, two approaches, as well as various combinations of them, exist.

One approach is based on the idea that certain elements of the philosophy should be developed before others. Thus, the development of auditory and visual discrimination and visual-motor skills might be considered to be of major importance in kindergarten, the development of word recognition skills stressed in the primary grades, followed by an emphasis on literal and simple interpretative meaning skills, and then critical-creative reading for pleasure. (Note, for example, many reading readiness programs could be used as total programs, followed by certain basal reader programs which are narrow in scope or even some linguistic programs, followed much later by wide reading.)

The other approach is based on the assumption that most or all of the elements should be developed from the beginning to the end and sequenced from simple to complex. Thus, from the beginning, materials must be interesting and varied. Literal, interpretative, and critical-creative skills are developed from the beginning, and children are taught where to locate appropriate materials; indeed, there is sufficient variety of materials available that such teaching becomes necessary.

Another point must be included here. The approach and/or the materials used in school may, in and of themselves, determine the sequence of skills that must be taught to the reader. Such is the case if the individualized reading approach is used: seeking, self-selection, and pacing. Such is the case when wide reading is used. And such may be the case when the language experience approach is used.

And certainly such is the case in reading in the content areas. As Bader (2) says, ". . . some content area specialists have come to understand that in guiding the reading-reasoning process in the printed materials of their discipline, they are teaching the skills of their discipline . . . . The goal is to produce content area teachers who will not see reading instruction as an added burden, or a remedial chore, but as an integral part of their effectiveness as instructors."

## Individual Differences among Students

Reading consultants, who guide teachers in their choice of materials and approaches, must be knowledgeable in implementing their philosophies of reading in terms of the wide range of mental ability and of reading achievement found in the typical classroom, as well as the wide range of interests and aspirations among individual students and groups of students.

The consultant should be able to teach the classroom teacher how to assess the needs and abilities of students by using standardized and informal techniques and how to locate materials appropriate to the needs and abilities of individuals or groups of students in terms of proper difficulty level, appropriate modal approach (for primary children), appropriate linguistic features, and desirable general approach (i.e., basal, modified orthographical, linguistic, language experience, etc.; in content areas, textbook, unit, modular, personalized, etc.).

Additionally, the consultant should guide teachers in becoming more knowledgeable about ways of assessing and enriching interests and aspirations in and through reading in all classrooms. The consultant should be able to guide teachers in locating materials and identifying approaches to satisfy and extend these interests and aspirations.

## Individual Differences among Teachers

Consultants should avoid rigidity in following an outlined program or a prototypic guide by trying to force teachers into a mold. Though such a guide may be helpful and, indeed, necessary, strict adherence to it will frequently destroy a possible *joie de vivre* in the classroom.

The best of teachers may use divergent approaches successfully. The consultant should recognize such excellence and encourage creativity. Poorer teachers will need much more guidance, and their divergence may lead to catastrophe. The consultant must know the difference, lest one lose the best teachers and afford too little guidance for the poorer ones.

## Change Agents

Reading consultants should serve as guides in a continuous evaluation of the reading program from K-12 in all areas of the curriculum. Such evaluation should be accomplished by using standardized tests, but the stress probably should be on informal techniques, including the use of informal reading inventories in the cognitive, affective, and psychomotor domains; classroom observations; conferences; and retrospective and introspective techniques.

Such evaluation should lead to strengthening the present program where it has proved to be successful and to altering it where it has not.

Reading consultants should keep abreast of current research and development and should serve as agents of change when results of research suggest promising new approaches to reading. They also should keep abreast of research methodology, and they should serve as leaders in researching promising approaches to reading in their school system.

## Selection of Reading Consultants

To provide for wide representation in the selection of a reading supervisor, or coordinator of reading consultants, the following plan is proposed:

A search committee composed of a representative group of principals of elementary and secondary schools and of consultants in the content area and of remedial reading teachers should recommend to the superintendent a candidate for the position of supervisor of reading. The supervisor should, thereafter, serve as chairman of the search committee to select consultants to fill various posts. Leaders of those concerned with that post should serve as members of the search committee.

Because there are relatively few people prepared to serve as reading consultants, search committees might identify promising teachers who should be encouraged to pursue the reading specialist program at a university which offers sufficient course work in the area. According to IRA standards (9), such work includes completion of the qualifications for the Special Teacher of Reading and, in addition,

1. an advanced course in the remediation and diagnosis of reading and learning problems;
2. an advanced course in the developmental aspects of a reading program;
3. a course, or courses, in curriculum development and supervision;
4. a course and/or experience in public relations; and
5. field experiences under a qualified reading consultant or supervisor in a school setting.

Recommendations for becoming a Reading Supervisor include additional courses in administrative procedures.

### References and Notes

1. Artley, A. Sterl. "Implementing a Developmental Reading Program on the Secondary Level," in Margaret Early (Ed.), *Reading Instruction in Secondary Schools*, Perspectives in Reading #2. Newark, Delaware: International Reading Association, 1964, 1-16.

2. Bader, Lois A. "Preparing Future Secondary Teachers in Reading," *Journal of Reading*, April 1972, 492-495.

3. Barrett, Thomas C. "Goals of a Reading Program: The Basis for Evaluation," in Thomas C. Barrett (Ed.), *The Evaluation of Children's Reading Achievement*, Perspectives in Reading #8. Newark, Delaware: International Reading Association, 1967, 13-26.

4. Burmeister, Lou E. "Objectives and Sources in Training Reading Specialists," *Journal of Reading*, October 1971, 54-59.

5. Clymer, Theodore L. "What Is 'Reading'?: Some Current Concepts," *Innovation and Change in Reading Instruction*, NSSE, 67th Yearbook, Part II. Chicago: University of Chicago Press, 1968, 7-29.

6. Early, Margaret. "About Successful Reading Programs," in M. Jerry Weiss (Ed.), *Reading in the Secondary Schools*. New York: Odyssey Press, 1961, 415-427.

7. Harris, T. L., Wayne Otto, and Thomas Barrett. "Summary and Review of Investigations Relating to Reading," *Journal of Educational Research*, February or March, yearly.

8. Mingoia, Edwin. "Improving the Reading of Academically Untalented Students," in M. Jerry Weiss (Ed.), *Reading in the Secondary Schools*. New York: Odyssey Press, 1961, 167-175.

9. See "Minimum Standards for the Professional Training of Reading Specialists" from the Professional Standards and Ethics Committee of the International Reading Association. Newark, Delaware: International Reading Association.

10. Simpson, Elizabeth A. "Organizing for Reading Instruction in the Secondary School," in Margaret Early (Ed.), *Reading Instruction in Secondary Schools*, Perspectives in Reading #2. Newark, Delaware: International Reading Association, 1964, 17-30.

11. Waples, Douglas. *What Reading Does to People.* Chicago: University of Chicago Press, 1968.

12. Weintraub, Samuel, et al. "Summary of Investigations Relating to Reading," *Reading Research Quarterly*, Issue 3, annually.

13. Whipple, Gertrude. "Characteristics of a Sound Reading Program," *Reading in the Elementary School*, NSSE, 48th Yearbook, Part II. Chicago: University of Chicago Press, 1949, 34-38.

# ONE VIEWPOINT ON PREPARING TEACHERS
# OF REMEDIAL READING

*Ned D. Marksheffel*
*Oregon State University*

Emphasis on one approach in methods of teaching and evaluation in preparing teachers of remedial reading at the master's level is preferable to that of teaching students a number of methods.

## Background

In attempting to improve their own teaching, professionals in the area of reading are constantly questioning their approaches and those of their colleagues in preparing teachers of reading. At times, the discussions confuse students and teachers because the discussants fail to define their terms. It, therefore, appears prudent and necessary to: 1) define the term *remedial reader* as used here; 2) determine what teachers of reading, administrators, parents, and pupils with reading problems expect of a remedial reading specialist; and 3) indicate the kinds of educational preparation that will adequately prepare the remedial reading specialist to meet the demands of all persons involved with remedial readers.

## Remedial Reader Defined

In this paper, a remedial reader is defined as one who is so severely retarded in reading that he is unable to achieve successfully in other academic areas in which reading is required for learning. A remedial reader has neurological and/or psychological problems in addition to the same kind of problems that afflict the retarded or corrective reader. He, therefore, requires the individualized help of a reading specialist or teacher.

Kress (5) notes that a remedial reader has an associative learning problem. He cannot associate the printed symbol with meaning from his own experiential background because he is unable to pronounce the written word. He cannot recognize, for example, a word such as *house* even though he has seen it and pronounced it with a teacher's help only seconds ago. Kress further states that the remedial reader's primary problem is nearly always one of learning to recognize words, and most authorities will agree on this point.

## What is Expected of a Remedial Reading Specialist?

Succinctly stated, administrators, teachers, parents, and the children who are remedial readers expect that the remedial reading specialist will teach the child how to read. They are not concerned with the causal factors contributing to the child's problem nor the development of specific reading skills necessary for him to read at his own potential. They simply want the child to learn to read.

Those who prepare the remedial reading specialist expect him to be competent to 1) diagnose with reasonable accuracy the child's strengths and weakness in reading, 2) obtain information about the child's reading potential, 3) have some valid idea of his intelligence, 4) provide individualized instruction that will help the child to successfully develop specific reading skills, 5) help the child to be aware of his own instructional needs and goals, and 6) provide interesting materials that will challenge the child's learning abilities but not overwhelm him in the process.

The remedial reading specialist, however, cannot be concerned solely with remediation. He must be vitally concerned with the prevention of severe reading problems among all children. There is nothing he can do about neurological difficulties or brain damage that is already present. He can, however, prevent psychological problems associated with reading failure. He can, for example, 1) diagnose children for classroom teachers, 2) help teachers develop reading lessons at children's instructional levels of learning instead of frustrating many of them by trying to teach all of them at the same level, 3) demonstrate how to teach children at various levels of reading, and 4) demonstrate how to teach various reading skills needed by individual children or groups of children.

## Preparation of Remedial Reading Specialists

The preceding minimal list of what is expected of a remedial reading specialist is sufficiently complex as it stands but is only an indicator of some of the major concerns of the remedial reading specialist. Is it any wonder that those who prepare specialists are concerned with the educational programs they follow?

Most institutions that grant a master's degree in remedial reading meet the *Minimum Standards of Professional Training of Reading Specialists* developed and published by the International Reading

Association. Some institutions exceed the suggested minimal standards.

It is interesting to compare the limited number of actual reading courses that are offered by most degree-granting institutions with their offering of supporting courses such as measurement and/or evaluation, psychology, adolescent and/or child psychology, the exceptional child, the maladjusted child, the mentally retarded child, linguistics, individualized intelligence testing, guidance, speech, and hearing.

The remedial reading program at Oregon State University is similar to a majority of programs at other universities and colleges, according to the courses listed in their catalogs. The required reading courses at the master's level for preparing remedial reading specialists totals 18 quarter hours. Because of the limited number of instructional reading hours, two questions are pertinent: "What kinds of courses in evaluation and teaching techniques should have priority?" and "Is it better to teach a limited number of concepts and skills in depth or try to cover a greater number of concepts, methods, and techniques?"

The program finally decided upon consists of the following reading courses: The Psychology of Reading, Diagnostic Techniques, Remedial Reading Procedures, and three quarters of Clinical Practicum, one quarter of the three being spent in supervised work in the public schools. In these courses, emphasis is given to developing a basic foundation group of transferable skills, techniques, and concepts of reading in three areas: evaluation and diagnosis, a directed reading lesson, and an adaptation of the Fernald-Keller technique (2).

## The Informal Reading Inventory

The Informal Reading Inventory (IRI) is the basic evaluative and diagnostic instrument. Students do have instruction, assigned reading and projects in working with various standardized tests of reading, the telebinocular and the reading eye.

The IRI, originally developed by Betts (1), in the writer's opinion, is the best diagnostic instrument available. It has its critics (and sometimes rightfully so) but the criticisms deal primarily with minor technicalities and not the principles upon which the IRI is based. Betts has stated many times that the greatest strengths and weaknesses of the IRI are in the competency of its user. The IRI makes it possible for the examiner to obtain insights into the extremely complex thinking processes of reading that would otherwise remain undiscovered.

One of the recognized major values of the IRI is that it makes it possible for the teacher to determine the level at which a pupil can read successfully and to provide him with adequate materials at this level.

In the course of determining a pupil's reading levels, numerous specific problems are uncovered. Phonic weaknesses, for example, can be spotted immediately. There is no guesswork about a child's being able or unable to pronounce words beginning with *str* blends or to recognize the *oi* diphthong. Nor is there any question about his ability to use context clues, read for meaning, associate meaning with certain vocabulary words, or benefit from silent reading before rereading orally. He is evaluated in a functional reading situation that is almost identical to his normal reading.

But the IRI yields other pertinent information to those who know how to use it. The alert examiner may observe symptoms of problems with vision, hearing, and speech that might be overlooked in a regular classroom.

Indications of the depth and variety of a child's thinking are revealed by his answers to questions. Some indication of his personality is revealed by the way in which he works in answering a question or trying to pronounce an unknown word. Does he quit immediately if he is unsure of his answer or pronunciation, or does he say, "Let me get it. Let me get it."

One could give numerous other specific examples of data that can be obtained by using an IRI, but these few samples should be indicative of the value of this instrument.

One of the major values of the IRI that has received only scant attention is its tremendous value in helping teachers and prospective teachers to better understand the reading behavior of pupils, to note how a child reacts when he finally achieves a goal successfully, or how he reacts to failure and frustration. The writer finds it to be an outstanding teaching-learning instrument for his students. Those who prefer to read more about the IRI might start with reading Betts (*1*), Johnson and Kress (*4*), Kress (*5*), and Marksheffel (*6*).

## A Directed Reading Lesson

There are several valid reasons for emphasizing the use of a directed reading lesson (DRL).

1. The general principles upon which the DRL is based are educationally and psychologically sound and can be applied to almost any kind of learning activity, especially those in which written materials are used, if the user understands it completely. What learning activity does not include some kind of readiness, purpose, use of specific vocabulary, comprehension checks, review, and enrichment or refinement of learned skills?

2. When the general pattern of a DRL is followed, it has tremendous potential for developing critical reading skills and critical thinking.

3. Properly used, it is an excellent evaluation instrument as well as a teaching device. With several minor exceptions, the DRL serves the purpose of and is similar to an informal reading inventory. While using it, the knowledgeable teacher continuously evaluates and diagnoses both the effectiveness of his teaching and the development of learning skills of each individual. And isn't the development of learning skills the goal of all teachers, regardless of materials, methods, and techniques used?

## The Fernald-Keller Technique

The Fernald-Keller technique, often called VAKT, was developed and used by Fernald (2), with the help of Helen Keller, in California in the early 1920s. It is not a panacea for all word-learning problems and should never be used indiscriminately with all pupils. When using the technique, most remedial readers can learn to recognize words that they were previously unable to learn.

It was noted previously that the remedial reader is unable to learn words through the usual visual-auditory approach. The remedial reader must have the additional help of the kinesthetic and tactile modes for learning words.

A competent remedial reading specialist can teach needed phonetic skills, syllabication, the transfer of learned syllables to unknown words, and structural clues to a remedial reader as he uses this method.

## Summary

Because it is impossible to teach even the most apt learner at the master's level all he needs to know about the reading processes, it appears to be a sound approach to teach the remedial reading specialist a basic foundation group of transferable skills, techniques, and concepts of reading that will prepare him to continue to learn and to develop on his own.

It is not the intent of this paper to imply that the suggested program of preparing remedial reading specialists is the only answer to better preparation of remedial reading teachers. It is hoped that the point of view taken will raise questions and perhaps will provide further insight and understanding in helping all children to become better readers.

**References**

1. Betts, Emmett A. *Foundations of Reading Instruction*. New York: American Book, 1957.

2. Fernald, Grace M. *Remedial Techniques in Basic School Subjects*. New York: McGraw-Hill, 1944.

3. Harris, Albert J. *How to Increase Reading Ability* (5th ed.). New York: David McKay, 1970.

4. Johnson, Marjorie Seddon, and Roy A. Kress. *Informal Reading Inventories*, Reading Aids Series. Newark, Delaware: International Reading Association, 1965.

5. Kress, Roy A. "When is Remedial Reading Remedial?" *Education*, 80 (May 1960), 540-544.

6. Marksheffel, Ned D. *Better Reading in the Secondary School*. New York: Ronald Press, 1966.

# PREPARING SPECIALIZED READING PERSONNEL FOR CENTRAL OFFICE POSITIONS

*Richard J. Smith*
*University of Wisconsin*

Each school district must determine which aspects of its total reading program can best be provided for at a central office level. That the needs and resources of school districts vary considerably, and that these differences should be reflected in central office organization and operation, is not to say that school districts have no commonalities in regard to reading curriculum development at the central office level. Sufficient similarity exists among school districts to recommend courses and supervised field experiences that are likely to be professionally useful for central office reading specialists in most school systems. The ideal is to provide courses and field experiences that are broad enough to permit the prospective specialist to draw upon his education to meet job specifications that vary from district to district.

Universities and colleges that prepare central office reading specialists can often approach the ideal in course work better than they can approach the ideal in field experiences. Books and journals that contain reports of the needs and the programs in school systems throughout the nation are available for study in courses and can help give students a broad picture of existing conditions. Such matter will thus complement the field experiences which must often be provided in public school systems geographically near the training institutions. Field experiences are more likely, therefore, to teach students how a particular school district is utilizing its central office staff to solve unique problems than to provide a good sampling of central office operations. For example, a student who has a field experience in the central office of the Madison, Wisconsin, public schools may learn little that is applicable to the most pressing problems of the New York public school system.

The recommendation, then, is that trainers of prospective central office reading specialists make special efforts to provide course work that includes some study of various school district operations in conjunction with field experiences that may be quite provincial in focus. Another possibility, of course, is to arrange field experiences in the same or in school districts similar to those in which the prospective specialist desires to obtain a position. Obviously, going out of the local area places additional burdens on the student and on supervisory personnel.

## Course Work

Students who are preparing themselves to assume reading specialist responsibilities at a central office level should have had the course work required or desired of the personnel for whom they will be instructional leaders; namely, the basic developmental and remedial reading courses that are offered to teachers or building consultants in elementary, secondary, or adult reading programs. In addition, the following courses would seem particularly relevant for central office reading specialists.

*Curriculum theory.* This course should consider different theoretical models and assumptions for curriculum development. Current writings and leading authorities in curriculum development should be studied.

*Statistical analysis and design in educational research.* This course should give some attention to designing and interpreting educational research as well as some introductory work with statistical procedures.

*Dynamics of instructional groups.* The content for this course should include research and theory on structures and processes of small groups with implications for teaching-learning procedures in small instructional groups. A desirable aspect of this course would be some encounter-group experiences to help the prospective specialist analyze his own interpersonal behavior.

*Administrator behavior.* The emphases in this course should be the role of administrators as instructional leaders and the nature and process of supervision for the improvement of instruction.

*Guiding and directing the school reading program.* This course should focus upon specific aspects of reading program development that need constant attention (e.g., the utilization of specialized personnel, inservice education in reading, evaluating instructional materials, school and classroom organization for reading instruction, evaluating the reading program, and evaluating individual pupil growth in the program). This course should also include the study of reading program developments throughout the nation as they are reported in the professional literature.

Certainly other courses would be helpful, but the five described here are especially good adjuncts to reading methods courses given to classroom teachers and special teachers of reading. The specific course descriptions will, of course, vary from institution to institution; but courses similar to those that are suggested seem desirable for most, if not all, central office reading specialists. The recommended courses may be taken prior to assuming the responsibilities of a central office job or as inservice education.

Since the responsibilities of central office specialists do vary from district to district, inservice course work would seem to be of utmost importance for central office personnel. Some school districts may see research as the major function of central office personnel. When such is the case, additional course work in research techniques and statistical analysis might be taken as inservice education. Other school districts may want their central office personnel primarily to provide inservice experiences for classroom teachers or to supervise classroom instruction. Additional course work to prepare central office specialists for these duties could be taken while personnel are on the job. The training of central office reading specialists, then, extends beyond preservice education. Central office personnel are instructional leaders and as such must accept the responsibility for staying in the forefront of their profession. Inservice education is necessary, therefore, for them to acquire the abilities needed for particular job responsibilities and to keep abreast of the developments in the field of reading and in fields related to reading curriculum development.

In regard to the course work taken while they are in service, it has been the writer's observation that central office reading specialists want to play an active role in the conduct of their classes. Specialists are generally aware of class needs and want to focus their reading, class discussion, and project work upon them; consequently, problem-centered discussion sessions with certain prerequisites for student enrollment are generally preferred. The prerequisites for student enrollment are suggested because students who are far below the sophistication level of most practicing central office specialists may be overwhelmed, bored, or both by the content of the discussions and the terminology employed. This is not to say that these courses should be reserved exclusively for practicing central office reading specialists. Students who are nearing that level of learning and experience can profit and contribute much when they are encouraged to participate in class interactions. The instructor of the course does, however, need to guard against the intimidation of less-experienced students by the enthusiasm and expertise of the more experienced.

Students from educational fields other than reading often add much to courses designed primarily for reading specialists. School psychologists, principals, researchers, librarians, and other specialists add points of view and information that can be extremely enlightening to central office reading specialists. At the same time the students representing fields other than reading will be helped to acquire understandings and insights that will ultimately result in more harmonious working relationships between reading specialists and specialists in related fields.

## Field Experiences

The value of supervised field experiences for prospective central office reading specialists cannot be overemphasized. Concerning the education of reading specialists, Austin (1) says, "Because the consultant is expected to assist inexperienced teachers as well as experienced ones, he should be required to complete a graduate practicum in a public school situation, in which he would work with a 'master' reading consultant. In this way he could combine theory with practice by obtaining first-hand knowledge of the problems encountered in the teaching of reading." Central office specialists, because of the broad scope of their responsibilities, will often benefit not only from field experiences in the central office itself but also from field experiences in clinics, school buildings, and classrooms which will ultimately come within the range of their responsibilities. Instructional leaders are always more effective when they have had some practical experience in the specific areas they are attempting to improve. Field experiences, therefore, should be arranged to give prospective specialists work experiences in as many aspects of a total district's reading program as possible. Most aspirants to central office positions already have a background of specialized work in reading, but field experiences which enrich and broaden their backgrounds are almost always needed.

Although much can be learned by observing the work of a practicing central office reading specialist, the emphasis of field experiences should be upon active participation in both the decision-making and implementation processes of program development. No two people work alike, and the specialist in training needs to develop his own style. He needs to plan his approach, grapple with the task, and receive evaluative feedback from his supervisors and the teachers or administrators with whom he has worked directly. Feedback from the teachers or administrators with whom he has worked is especially valuable. To assure honest and helpful feedback, university supervisors should make it clear to all that students taking field experiences are not expected to be finished products. By the same token, students must understand that honest criticism of their efforts is a major part of every field experience. Students who complete a field experience without an honest appraisal of their work from the principal people involved miss a helpful dimension of their field experience.

University supervisors, public school personnel, and the specialist in training should all participate in deciding upon and arranging the specifics of each field experience. Factors which enter into the decisions that are made are the needs of the practicum student and the opportunities available in public schools at that particular time. At the University of Wisconsin the practice of assigning practicum students to projects that are currently in operation and giving the students carefully delineated responsibilities within those projects has been found to work well. One must always be careful, however, to allow room for some decision-making on the part of the student within his assignment. For example, one doctoral candidate was assigned to help central office staff members in Madison initiate a teacher aide program designed to enable teachers to give corrective readers more help. With the help of a central office consultant, the practicum student was required to plan and conduct inservice programs for teachers and aides, select instructional materials, and communicate the progress of the project to principals and other central office staff. Another practicum student undertook the responsibility for providing several inservice programs to teachers in three rural elementary schools in Wisconsin. The student had to meet and plan with the principals and other district administrators as well as observe the teachers at work and offer helpful suggestions to them at their after-school meetings. Still another student worked with the members of the science department in a Madison senior high school to help construct, administer, and interpret informal reading inventories for students. This project required coordination with the reading consultant employed in that particular high school.

Although it is sometimes tempting to use practicum students to perform relatively unsophisticated tasks at the central office level, these temptations should be resisted. Finding responsibilities that are challenging without being overwhelming is not always easy, but every attempt should be made to see that the student has experiences at or near his level of sophistication. Sometimes short-term projects can be arranged which meet the student's needs and are beneficial to the general interests of the central office reading department. Inservice education that is offered to a selected group of teachers and is relevant to a specific aspect of reading instruction can often be used effectively to give the prospective central office specialist the experience he needs in teacher education and at the same time improve one dimension of the district reading program.

## Conclusion

The basic principles that apply to the training of other reading specialists apply also to the training of central office reading personnel. Because of the broader range of responsibilities that fall under the central office "umbrella" and the variety of organizational structures and operating procedures from district to district, it is more difficult to delineate a specific program of preparation. Perhaps the major difference between central office positions and other positions of specialization is that personnel in the central office are farther away from the students for whom their services are ultimately intended. The transition from a school building, where daily contacts with students provide much job satisfaction to the central office where the impact of one's work is often not visible, can be difficult. People making the transition must be given assurance that their new positions are needed and wanted and do bear fruit although it sometimes appears otherwise. Not everyone who aspires to a central office reading position finds the job satisfactory when he samples it. The training program leading to central office specialization, therefore, should be looked upon as an opportunity to decide whether the trainee is suited to that level of specialization. The training period should be perceived by all who are involved in the training as a testing as well as a preparatory process.

## Reference

1. Austin, Mary C. "Professional Training of Reading Personnel," *Innovation and Change in Reading Instruction*, the 67th Yearbook of the National Society for the Study of Education. Chicago: University of Chicago Press, 1968, 357-396.

# COMPUTER SIMULATION FOR TRAINING EDUCATIONAL DIAGNOSTICIANS

*Janet W. Lerner*
*Northwestern University*

Simulation is described as a procedure in which a model or an analog to a real life situation is created for the purpose of testing or teaching. A systems analyst seeks to construct a model or definition of a system that is realistic and corresponds to reality in certain relevant particulars. Thus a simulation duplicates certain activities of a system without attaining reality itself.

Simulation procedures are increasingly recognized as effective techniques in education. In a 1970 report to Congress, the Commission on Instructional Technology forecasts that simulation is likely to become the most important educational development of the decade.

The use of computer simulation as a technique in education has been scarcely explored. Simulated games have been widely used in the fields of business management and military science to promote more efficient decision making, to better understand the system under study, to analyze the relationship of the elements within the system, and to test certain decision making rules. Computer simulations permit practice in business management decisions without the risk of bankruptcy; they allow military decision making to be practiced without the loss of life or actual battles; and they permit prospective medical specialists to make diagnostic and therapeutic decisions without endangering the health of patients. The success found with this technique in many disciplines suggests that the technology could be adapted to the field of reading.

The field of reading, however, has been scarcely touched by the powerful and adaptable technology of the computer. There have been few applications of the computer to the field of reading other than the use of statistical library programs to analyze data in research studies. Most students preparing to be reading specialists and researchers are not exposed to computer technology. The potential of computer simulation procedures, as well as other computer applications in the field of reading, has been virtually unexplored.

### The Computer Feasibility Study

In the Northwestern University Learning Disabilities Program, a feasibility study was conducted to explore and develop ways of applying computer technology to reading and learning disabilities and to train specialists who are familiar with computer methods. A major facet of this investigation concerned the development of computer simulation programs as a method of training specialists in the process of diagnosing cases of reading and learning disabilities.

This simulation was designed to approximate the actual conditions of the diagnostic clinic at Northwestern University. The simulated and computerized child attended the clinic for the same length of time that children actually do attend the diagnostic clinic session; they were subject to similar tests, reports, and observations. The clinic staff actually met to plan, to develop hypotheses, to make decisions, to develop a diagnosis, and to recommend teaching procedures. This type of simulation has been referred to as an operational simulation, ". . . a simulation within operational environments, in which human participants use their judgments and other human abilities to interact with the simulated system" (1).

A primary aim of the reading and learning disabilities programs in colleges and universities is to train prospective specialists to make a diagnosis of a child with a suspected reading disability and to plan and implement remediation within a clinical teaching program. The process of diagnosing and teaching is a continuous, dynamic process requiring the intercorrelation of many elements and variables, including tests, observations, medical reports, and case histories. The selection of data, the functions to be tested, the follow-up procedures, the hypothesis formulation concerning the nature of the problem, the recommendations and referrals, and the development of a teaching plan are among the decisions that must be made.

Typically, the diagnostic teaching process is discussed in a theory course and the student gains experience while working with children in a clinic or practicum course. Students generally find such clinic experiences extremely valuable. Unfortunately, this clinic practice is often limited within the training program because of the costs involved. For the following reasons clinical experiences are frequently inadequate to train reading specialists: clinic space is often limited, college supervisory personnel is in short supply, student time that can be devoted to clinic work is insufficient, and mistakes made in diagnosing and teaching may be detrimental to the child involved. Computer simulation can provide one way to supplement and enrich training experiences for the reading disabilities specialist. Simulation is, thus, one way to bridge the gap between the theory course and the clinical experiences. It is not intended to be a substitute for either, but it does provide additional experiences without the expense and difficulties involved in the clinical setting.

### The Simulated Diagnostic Computer Game

The simulation procedure was used as an integral part of a graduate course in diagnosis. This project used a computer simulation game approach to enable the participants (students in the course) to practice diagnostic decision making. Extensive information on a specific child with reading disabilities was stored in computer memory. Students were organized into several diagnostic teams, each consisting of about five staff members. Each team made a series of decisions concerning the simulated case. Diagnostic decision making requires that specialists arrive at decisions concerning case history, observations, and tests. Realistically, certain constraints limit data collection within any organizational setting, and these constraints affect decisions. Constraints include variables such as time, money, and facilities. Some of these constraints were built into the simulation program.

For example, the scarce resource was time; each request or decision came at a cost of time. If Silent Reading Test A was requested by the staff, the computer checked to find how long this particular test took to administer and whether sufficient time remained in the diagnostic session to give it. If insufficient time remained to give that particular test, the computer message in the printout would tell the team that the child had gone to lunch. The computer would also check to find whether another test that had been requested by the team could be given in the remaining time.

The teams participating in the computer simulation met for several staffing sessions to make decisions and request information from the computer. A computer printout based on their decisions was given to each member of the team at the next simulated staffing session. The routine of staffing sessions and computer printouts is diagramed in the flow chart shown in Figure 1. There were four staffing sessions: prestaffing, noonstaffing, poststaffing, and concluding session.

At the prestaffing, the team received preliminary information about the child: name, age, grade, and general problem. The teams were also given the information that could be obtained about the child from the computer. This information included scores from a

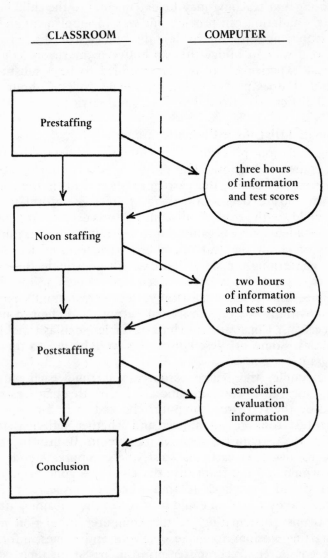

**Figure 1.** Flowchart of the Simulated Diagnosis

large variety of tests. Total scores or subtest scores could be obtained. In addition, medical, neurological, EEG, ophthalmological, or psychiatric reports could be requested. Other possible information included teacher behavior reports, case history data, and speech and language reports. Each piece of information, however, was tied to a realistic time constraint. Since the morning diagnostic session was scheduled for the simulated time period of 9:00 a.m. to 12:00 noon, the computer would release only three hours of diagnostic information to a team. Thus, the prestaffing consisted of wisely planning the morning diagnostic session. Though each team was diagnosing the same simulated child, each team received different information because each team had made different diagnostic decisions.

At the simulated noonstaffing, the teams received computer printouts of the morning decisions and planned for two hours of additional diagnostic examinations (1:00 p.m. to 3:00 p.m.). At this session, the teams were beginning to develop hypotheses concerning the child's problem, and the afternoon session was planned to test or substantiate these hypotheses.

At the poststaffing, the teams evaluated the information they had obtained during the simulated sessions and developed a series of diagnostic decisions. These included decisions such as determining the child's disability, his level of development, his strengths and weaknesses, whether referrals were necessary, and what teaching procedures were to be recommended. In addition, specific decisions were made concerning materials and methods. At the concluding staffing, each member received a printout showing the decisions made by all participating teams. At this session the entire class discussed the diagnostic decisions of the various teams.

Student reaction to this simulation project was enthusiastic. The students commented that the simulation: 1) required them to make decisions concerning tests, information from other professionals, and time allotments; 2) created a realistic, face-to-face staffing situation; 3) forced them to organize the data to develop hypotheses; and 4) permitted them to compare their decisions with those made by other diagnostic teams.

## Implications

The results of this pilot study suggest that computer simulation is a promising technique for the training of specialists in the diagnostic teaching process. This simulation was only one area of computer application in a project designed to introduce computer technology to prospective reading and learning disabilities specialists. In addition, students learned the computer language FORTRAN, wrote and ran programs on the CDC 6400 computer at the Northwestern University Vogelback Computer Center, and developed computer applications to the problems faced while working with children with reading and learning disabilities. Since specialists are likely to find themselves in career positions in hospitals, schools, and clinics that have unused computer capacity available, such training should prove to be very valuable.

A number of procedures are being studied at present to improve and enrich the computer simulation. Students need exposure to various types of disability cases, and a bank of various types of cases could be collected and stored on computer tape. If the program is put on an "on-line computer terminal" facility, the student can give one test at a time and receive immediate feedback to help him make his next decision. It might be possible to provide additional realism in the simulation by providing videotape of the child during the testing and recording of his performance.

It has been said that the fastest diagnostic method is a shrewd guess. The question arises as to how the investigator makes this shrewd guess. Does he pull it out of thin air? Is there a guide? Are there any procedures that will improve his ability to make a good guess?

The initiate needs logical and methodological aids to help him develop such skills. The goals of the simulated diagnosis are to enhance the diagnostic skills of the investigator, sensitize him to critical symptoms, give practice in the skill of closure while coping with many variables, and give experience in team staffing and group decision making.

**Reference**

1. Hare, Van Court, Jr. *Systems Analysis: A Diagnostic Approach*. New York: Harcourt, Brace and World, 1967, 366.

# THE ROLE OF THE SECONDARY SCHOOL
# READING CONSULTANT

*M. Bernice Bragstad*
*LaFollette High School*
*Madison, Wisconsin*

Have you ever thought of evolution as being related to the role of the secondary school reading consultant? Evolution is defined as "a series of related changes in a certain direction." The primary function of the reading consultant is to work with teachers in effecting changes in attitudes, in methods, and in curriculums so that all students move toward their full potentials in learning. This evolutionary aspect of related changes in a certain direction must be a continuous process if there is to be progressive development of the school's reading program.

## Detecting the Thinking Process

For some teachers the first change is to conceive of reading not as a subject in itself but as a thinking process that differs with the subject matter being studied. For example, consider Martian course in "spyloctogy" for a fresh look at the nature of mathematics, as was done in geometry classes at LaFollette High School. A detailed description follows to illustrate an approach applicable for teachers in other content areas. Mathematics teachers think it has made them more aware of process and its relationship to understanding content. Notice what causes difficulty in understanding spyloctogy and what thinking processes are required.

### An Example from Martian Mathematics
### Taken from a Text in Spyloctogy (1)

In this chapter, we will be concerned with a study of the Pexlomb. A Pexlomb is defined as any Zox with pictanamerals which flotate the Zox into five berta Zubs where each Zub is supramatilate to the Rosrey of the Ord. For example, consider the Zox defined by 3 berta Ooz. It is obvious that any pictanameral which is Blat must necessarily be Cort to the Ord. This follows from our knowledge of the relationship of a dentrex to its voom. However, if the Ord is partivasimous then the Zox must be Zubious. Thus if we kizate the dox pictanameral, our Zox will be flotated into 5 berta zubs. But remember, each zub must be supramatilated to the Rosrey of the Ord. If any one of the zubs is not supramatilated, we then have a pixilated Pexlomb which requires a completely different procedure.

We can represent the necessary conditions by the following:

1. Q??---¢ (note: Q is nubbed according to the principle of Plasimony)
2. By Axdrellation we arrive at: X Q/??---!!-* Thus, it is evident that the solution must be:
3. M---/?? (Really quite simple if you remember to obscone in step 4 of the Axdrellation process.)

What becomes apparent in this example?

1. The student must know the various kinds of vocabulary.
2. The student must be able to see the relationship of abstractions—X to Q, the dentrex to its voom. Exactly what is the relationship when "each Zub is supramatilate to the rosrey of the Ord"?
3. The student must hold ideas and relationships in suspension as he continues to deal with more relationships and more information in the problem. The words "Thus it is evident" anticipate the synthesis of all this thinking in the solution of the problem—a very complex, abstract thinking process.
4. The students must realize that mathematics is dense, often packed with many concepts in a few sentences. As a result the student must read slowly—and then reread. Speed and comprehension are negatively related in mathematics.
5. Finally, a student must recognize the cumulative nature of mathematics with its concepts on an increasing scale of difficulty.

## Understanding the Mind

After perceiving the nature of mathematics and the thinking processes involved, a relevant question may be: Since all this complex, abstract thinking is done by the brain, what do we know about this ten-billion celled instrument that can help us teach students how to learn more effectively? We know that complete understanding is essential to remembering. We know that frequent use or review of new material facilitates retention. We know that in a cumulative subject, gaps in understanding bring the mind to a standstill until meaning fills that gap. We know that attitudes affect the functioning of the mind. For example, a positive attitude coupled with intellectual curiosity causes the mind to be more effective in comprehension; asking questions is a sign of brainpower and is basic to learning.

If one had a computer with ten billion parts, one would need directions in how to use it. So, too, in mathematics or any content area, the student must synthesize his understanding of the nature of that subject and his knowledge of the mind's functioning into a workable plan for learning in that particular course.

### Developing Learning Strategy

When a student has realized the high level thinking skills he needs to understand mathematics, he feels the need for higher level study skills. Materials developed by Thomas (2) on study skills in geometry are an excellent resource for students when they are ready to develop their own learning strategies. From this material they discover how to learn vocabulary, how to do in-depth reading, how to attend to diagrams and figures, plus how to use other suggestions for understanding mathematics.

After the students have studied this material, the teacher asks each student to write a personal evaluation of what he must do to learn effectively in mathematics. This procedure includes the student's recording how his past study procedures must be changed to effect better learning.

Four weeks after the initial presentations, the teacher and reading consultant help the students evaluate their follow through by determining what specifics in their learning strategy have been helpful and what changes still need to be made. Students are then asked to write their honest reactions to the course and to make any suggestions that would facilitate learning for them. One student commented, "Since there is real follow up, we know you are serious about wanting to help us learn." The students were experiencing education as a cooperative process in which they had assumed some responsibility for growth and change. The teacher had acquired the necessary personal and intellectual flexibility to make use of feedback from students in adjusting instruction. As a result, an atmosphere of honest interaction between consultant and teacher and between teacher and students made learning meaningful for everyone involved.

### Helping the Disabled Learner

If all students are to be helped, the disabled learner must also receive the consultant's attention. Too often for this student, reading is not a means of learning but a frustrating end in itself. Teachers often have difficulty accepting these students as they are and setting reasonable behavioral objectives in working with them. A perceptive western civilization team of teachers realized, however, that they must know a student's strengths and weaknesses before knowing what to teach and how to teach disabled learners. The three teachers administered an oral reading test, detected the most common errors, and recorded the results. The oral reading test used was an informal inventory based on social studies materials at various levels. Although it took three days to finish testing all students individually, the teachers felt they had established a rapport with the students that ordinarily would have taken many weeks to develop. While talking to the students in testing, the teachers learned each student's interests and concerns; subsequently, the curriculum which was created could be meaningful. The students felt they had a part in developing the course and appreciated the personal attention.

Later, the reading consultant helped in evaluating teacher-made materials and games developed to motivate the students to read. Thus, with the western civilization team, the reading consultant's role was to equip the teachers in diagnosing problems, interpreting data, and then assisting in adequate instructional adjustment.

## Making Corrective Reading Meaningful

An American history team at LaFollette High School begins the semester by diagnosing students' needs with the following:

1. The Nelson-Denny test with an item analysis so the teacher and students know what skills each student needs to develop and what skills the entire class needs to develop.

2. An informal inventory on course material with questions asked to assess the comprehension and study skills of each student.

The teachers and the consultant then develop a card file with the diagnostic information recorded for approximately 600 juniors.

Each year this testing reveals the range within a class to be from about fifth grade level to college level. Since students cannot improve their reading skills when they are working at the frustration level, all materials available for the course are evaluated for difficulty of vocabulary, sentence length, concept load, and study helps. Each student knows his reading level and the level of all suggested material for a unit so he can intelligently choose what to read. Sometimes all students focus on the same questions or concepts but use different sources; at other times, the students have differentiated assignments. Meanwhile, the search continues for materials, both fiction and nonfiction, at a variety of levels for each unit in the course.

When the teachers in any content area realize the needs of their students in terms of specific skills, teachers begin to see improved reading skills as synonymous with improved learning in their subject. Then the reading consultant is in a position to be helpful. Some commercially prepared developmental reading materials are good resources for helping teachers understand what the reading skills are and what techniques can be used in developing these skills. With the help of the reading consultant, the teachers can adapt these techniques to course materials. The skill development program can then be ongoing and productive.

## Innovating Interdepartmental Cooperation

One other activity the writer wishes to illustrate is interdepartmental cooperation in helping students develop skills such as detecting the organizational structure of an article in reading or seeing the main concepts and how they are supported or developed. The science and history teachers are helped in giving their students practice in previewing and questioning before reading so the students have a mental map for guidance. To further reenforce this organizational skill, speech class becomes a laboratory for preparing, outlining, and practicing speeches to be given in the science and social studies classes on subjects related to units being studied. Point of view and critical thinking are emphasized when a single topic, such as the population explosion, is presented as a scientific problem in science and as a social issue in social studies. The listeners write down the main ideas. A reading consultant is in a unique position to facilitate this type of interdepartmental development of communications skills common to reading, listening, speaking, and writing. As a result, teachers and students become aware of the thinking processes common to learning in various content areas.

## Implementing the Reading Program

Other examples of reading consultant activities at LaFollette High School include: 1) helping teachers prepare materials to aid students in learning how to listen, how to take notes on lectures, how to write examinations, how to use SQ3R in the various content areas, and how to prepare for a laboratory experience in science; 2) assisting teachers in development of informal inventories in science, industrial arts, and social psychology; 3) helping teachers in the business department develop a vocabulary building program; 4) assisting the football coach in evaluating the study skills of the football team; 5) working with science, English, and social studies teachers in curriculum development; 6) directing inservice training for new teachers; 7) teaching a remedial reading course to teachers of disabled readers; 8) working with reading personnel K-12 in developing behavioral objectives for a continuous reading program at every level of education; 9) assisting in the development of a performance criterion testing program based on behavioral objectives within content areas; and 10) evaluating plans for effective testing. Of special interest is the development of a reading course negotiated by teachers and the board of education for all faculty and administrators who have not recently completed a reading course. Teachers and administrators are currently assessing their needs as a first step toward developing the reading course.

Sharing insights in working together is good inservice training for the consultant as well as for the teachers and administrators. When teachers see positive results of their attempts to improve student learning, those teachers are willing to share their ideas with the faculty on regular inservice days, with students in a university class to help prospective teachers see the application of theory to real teaching situations, and with parents at PTA meetings. Through such teacher involvement, the reading program becomes the teacher's program and not just that of the reading consultant.

### Creating the Consulting Relationship

Sampling teacher opinion, the writer discovered that teachers give top priority to four characteristics for a reading consultant: strong academic background, creativity, enthusiasm, and the capacity for personal relationship. Without the last quality, the capacity for personal relationship, the preceding attributes may be without effect. Working with people is the only way that a reading consultant can implement a reading program. Being an open, caring person is crucial in the consulting relationship. Teachers must feel that honest interaction is both desirable and acceptable; then the teachers and the consultant are in a position to experiment and learn together. To be a reading consultant is to be a person in relationship with others in a common pursuit—helping all students move toward their full potential in learning.

### References

1. Smith, Donald E. P. (Ed.). *Learning to Learn*. New York: Harcourt, Brace and World, 1961, 81.
2. Thomas, Ellen Lamar. *A Higher-Level Reading Approach for Geometry*, printed at the Laboratory Schools, University of Chicago.

# AN ECLECTIC APPROACH TO TRAINING

*Wayne Otto*
*University of Wisconsin*

A vast range of pupil characteristics, teacher attributes, and instructional approaches is both readily observable in the schools and frequently demonstrated in the literature. The position taken in this paper is that recognition of this diversity must be reflected in training programs for remedial teachers if the trainees are ever to cope successfully with their own strengths and limitations as well as with pupil idiosyncrasies in selecting and/or devising viable approaches to remedial instruction. Because teachers' attributes and childrens' problems differ and because we have not discovered—and, in the writer's opinion, will not discover in the foreseeable future— any universal cures for reading problems, we must take an eclectic approach to training in order to establish the flexibility that is required by the facts of life.

Frieder (3) gets it all together when he says: "Many alternatives are currently available to the prescriber in the area of media and strategies; but despite the advances in diagnosis and instruction, research has provided little concrete information about the prescriber's task—putting diagnosis and instruction together to reach objectives." A cynic might say that if we don't really know what we're doing, the only thing we *can* do is take an eclectic approach. But the writer prefers to "accentuate the positive" even though it may be impossible to "eliminate the negative." In another context (6), it was put this way: "We doubt that research-based knowledge relative to the systematic matching of pupils and materials/methods is forthcoming in the foreseeable future. . . . teachers will need to continue to make judgments regarding the instruction of individual pupils. Such judgments will best be made by sensitive teachers with clear perceptions of pupils' needs, explicit objectives, and knowledge of a wide range of methods and materials."

We may not be able to do much to make anyone sensitive; but we can help teachers-in-training to recognize diversity, to accept limitations, to establish objectives, to become familiar with a wide range of methods and materials, to question pat answers, and, ultimately, to take an eclectic, problem-solving approach to remedial teaching. *Eclectic* means ". . . not following any one system . . . but selecting and using what are considered the best elements of all systems." *That* is the desired approach after the training program is completed, for we have no evidence whatever to support any single system to the exclusion of all others. But if we want teachers to be in a position to take a creative, problem-solving approach to each case they encounter, then we must devise training programs that encourage such behavior as well as supply the basic knowledge required.

With the basic position stated, let us consider the rationale for an eclectic approach to remedial teaching; and then let us consider a training program designed to encourage eclecticism.

## Rationale

The only rationale needed for an eclectic approach is inherent in the following quotations.

James (5) put it this way more than half a century ago: "The art of teaching grew up in the classroom, out of inventiveness and sympathetic concrete observation. Even where . . . the advancer of the art was also a psychologist, the pedagogics and the psychology ran side by side, and the former was not derived in any sense from the latter. The two were congruent, but neither was subordinate. And so everywhere the teaching must *agree* with the psychology, but need not necessarily be the only kind of teaching that would so agree; for many diverse methods of teaching may equally well agree with psychological laws." That seems to be a clear invitation to eclecticism—not hit-or-miss eclecticism, but eclecticism based on diverse knowledge.

In her excellent article on individual differences, Tyler (8) makes this observation: ". . . it is psychological individuality which is of the greatest importance to education. Each student in a classroom, no matter how carefully selected as a member of a 'homogeneous' group, will of necessity react in his own unique way to the situation. There are differences in talents and aptitudes, in interests and motives, in habits and response styles, in emotional needs and vulnerabilities. In education as in medicine, there is really no 'norm.' When a teacher makes an assignment to a class of 30, it is actually 30 different assignments that are carried out." Most teachers would heartily agree with this opinion—even those who have never made a differentiated assignment in their lives. The message is very clear: No single approach or focus is likely to be adequate to deal with the vast range of individual differences in any school situation.

The latter point was also made quite vigorously by Bracht (2): "Bloom . . . Chronbach . . . Gagné . . . Glaser . . . Jensen . . . and other educational psychologists have suggested that no single instructional process provides optimal learning for all students. Given a common set of objectives, some students will be more successful with one instructional program and other students will be more successful with an alternative instructional program. Consequently, a greater proportion of students will attain the instructional objectives when instruction is differentiated for different types of students."

Bracht (2) also makes this statement on experimental factors related to aptitude-treatment interactions: "The goal of research on ATI (aptitude-treatment interactions) is to find significant disordinal interactions between alternative treatments and personological variables, i.e., to develop alternative instructional programs so that optimal educational payoff is obtained when students are assigned differently to alternative programs." Such research would hopefully and ultimately serve to provide guidelines for the systematic matching of pupils and treatments. Presently, however, the surface has barely been scratched. Until the scratch has been deepened considerably—and to get on with the task of identifying viable alternatives to be researched—we are well advised to maintain a repertoire of treatment options to be employed as they appear appropriate. And the name of the game is eclecticism—not hit-or-miss, trial-and-error fumbling, but careful selection of the treatment that appears to be most appropriate for a given pupil at a given point in time.

The selection of treatments for pupils is what Harris (4) is talking about in the introduction to his *Casebook on Reading Disability*: "A combination of teaching methods was used with most of these children, teaching visual recognition of common words while also teaching phonics, and devoting part of the lesson to oral and silent reading. The Gillingham method of phonics instruction was followed in Cases 4, 14, and 16, and was sometimes combined with kinesthetic procedures (Case 10). The Fernald kinesthetic or VAKT method was employed in several of the cases, usually with some modification. For example, in Case 2 the child's lack of fine motor control made writing difficult, so typing was substituted. A language experience approach utilizing the child's own dictation was employed at the beginning in several cases, at times combined with reading of easy printed material." He goes on, but the point is adequately made that careful case studies are likely to be the bases for a variety of approaches. Again, eclecticism is the name of the game. The point is that the rationale for an eclectic approach to both teaching and teacher training is implicit in what people who have considered the diversity in pupils and in teaching have had to say.

## A Training Program

What does all of this have to say about the training of remedial teachers? To the writer, the message is very clear: The training program should be based on a broad background of knowledge, and it should include a variety of practicum experiences.

Zedler (9) is not talking exclusively about remedial reading teachers, but her points are relevant here: ". . . the training for teachers of children who cannot learn by conventional procedures should not be a superimposed program, but should begin at the undergraduate level and proceed through a fifth year. The goal should be prevention rather than remediation; therefore, the teachers should be prepared to teach at the kindergarten and primary grade levels. Student-teachers should first acquire a broad eclectic background of knowledge from which they can develop frameworks for understanding: a) children who learn normally and those who do not, b) the nature of language, c) the process of learning itself, and d) the pathologies of language and learning. Out of such knowledge student-teachers should develop skills: a) in evaluating learning abilities; b) in regular, diagnostic, and therapeutic teaching; c) in relating to and strengthening the self-concepts of children with learning problems; d) in communicating with related professions; and e) in evaluating and participating in high quality research. During the development of these specific skills, student-teachers should be skillfully supervised by college and university professors with high degrees of competence in the areas they supervise."

Zedler's statement gets it all together regarding the need for an eclectic knowledge base. To her statement the writer would add his belief that realistic, meaningful, practicum experiences are most likely to take place in a school setting. Braam and Oliver (1) point out their feeling that a field experience for undergraduates in an elementary level reading course ". . . has contributed to a bridging of the gap between ivory tower and classroom." The need for bridging the credibility gap is even greater in graduate courses in remedial reading. Furthermore, the confrontation of real-world problems in a real-world setting helps to engender an independent, problem-solving approach to remedial teaching. And once again the name of the game is eclecticism!

With apologies for being provincial, the writer would like to describe briefly a couple of things done at the University of Wisconsin at Madison to provide realistic, eclectic field work experiences in a school setting. These efforts are possible only because of the cooperation and support of personnel in the Madison public schools. The description is excerpted from an article by Otto and Smith (7).

During the regular school year students in the university remedial reading course are able to work with elementary level pupils in the public schools within the framework of a school-university cooperative tutoring program. Of the three weekly course-contact hours, students spend two in a lecture-discussion session and one working with a child with moderate reading problems in the public schools. Thus, the students have an opportunity to become familiar with the techniques of assessment and remedial teaching in a naturalistic setting. They are required to prepare a written case report, which includes a tentative diagnosis, a prognostic statement in which they predict the rate and degree of progress that might realistically be expected in view of the facts in the case, and a proposed plan for continued instruction.

... A central office reading consultant coordinates the public school aspect of the program. She presents the program to the building principals, identifies the schools that will participate, and gives the university students an overview of the reading program in the public schools. Students are assigned only to schools that have the services of a reading resource teacher .... The reading resource teacher selects the child to be tutored, makes arrangements for the sessions, and generally guides the university student in selecting and using tests and materials. In most instances the weekly hour of tutoring is done in two half-hour sessions.

The remedial reading practicum that is offered during the regular school year is also tied to the public school program. Whereas the tutoring program is conceived mainly as a familiarization experience for university students, the practicum is conceived as an intensive, closely supervised experience. Therefore, to permit adequate supervision most of the students during any given semester are placed in a single school designated the "practicum school." ... each student works with one or two pupils with severe reading problems and gains experience in diagnosis, remedial teaching, and case reporting. The case report is, of course, passed on to the classroom teacher, who cooperates with the student in coordinating the remedial instruction with classroom instruction throughout the semester of practicum work.

The university practicum instructor has direct responsibility for supervision of the students; and the "practicum school" has a Title I supported remedial reading teacher, who is available as a resource person on a day-to-day basis. The remedial teacher works with pupils from grades one through three and the practicum students work with pupils from grades four through six, so there is a sharing of responsibilities for pupils who need remedial help. A reading consultant from the public school's central office staff makes regular visits to observe and supervise the school's overall remedial program. Diagnostic materials are supplied to the practicum students by the university, but most of the teaching materials are supplied by the school.

The university also offers a course titled Field Work in School Reading Programs during the regular school year. It differs from the practicum mainly in the fact that the focus is upon a school's overall reading program rather than upon individual pupils with problems in reading. The intent is to provide relevant field experience for students, usually at the post-master's level, who aspire to become reading consultants.

In the several aspects of the cooperative school-university program, these students see a wide variety of problems in a variety of settings and are encouraged to see also the wide variety of resources available and the variety of approaches that can be taken. Flip Wilson says, "What you see is what you get!" In this case, what you get is eclectic.

### References

1. Braam, Leonard S., and Marvin E. Oliver. "Undergraduate Reading Education," *Reading Teacher*, 23 (1970), 426-428.

2. Bracht, Glenn H. "Experimental Factors Related to Aptitude Treatment Interactions," *Review of Educational Research*, 40 (1970), 627-645.

3. Frieder, Brian. "Motivator: Least Developed of Teacher Roles," *Educational Technology*, 10 (1970), 28-36.

4. Harris, Albert J. *Casebook on Reading Disability*. New York: McKay, 1970.

5. James, William. *Talks to Teachers*. New York: Henry Holt, 1904.

6. Otto, Wayne, Richard A. McMenemy, and Richard J. Smith. *Corrective and Remedial Reading* (2nd Ed.). Boston: Houghton Mifflin, 1973.

7. Otto, Wayne, and Richard J. Smith. "School-University Cooperation in the Preparation of Reading Teachers," *Reading Teacher*, 24 (May 1971), 718-722.

8. Tyler, Leona E., "Individual Differences," in R. L. Ebel, V. H. Noll, and R. M. Bauer (Eds.), *Encyclopedia of Educational Research* (4th ed.). New York: Macmillan, 1969.

9. Zedler, Empress Y. "Better Teacher Training—The Solution for Children's Reading Problems," *Journal of Learning Disabilities*, 3 (1970), 106-112.

# ROLES OF CENTRAL OFFICE READING PERSONNEL

*George Jurata*
*Jefferson County, Colorado, Schools*

As stated by the IRA Professional Standards and Ethics Committee, personnel can be divided into two categories: those who work directly with children and those who work directly with teachers as consultants or supervisors with prime responsibility for developing and maintaining the district reading program (5). The focus of this paper is to discuss the roles and responsibilities of central office personnel charged with the responsibility for developing and maintaining a district reading program.

The job classifications most frequently found at the district level are reading coordinator, supervisor, reading consultant, or resource specialist. In most cases, the reading coordinator or supervisor assumes the total responsibility for the district reading program. He is usually directly responsible to the superintendent or to an assistant superintendent of instruction. District level reading consultants or reading specialists work with the reading coordinator and are usually responsible to him.

Few personnel are charged with overall responsibility for the district reading program (6). In spite of being few in number, however, this group is in a position to greatly influence the direction and quality of a school system's reading program. It is quite fitting, therefore, that considerable emphasis be given to the most efficient and productive avenues through which central office personnel approach their defined responsibilities.

## Major Responsibilities of the Reading Coordinator

Consistent with the IRA Professional Standards and Ethics Committee recommendations, reading coordinators and resource specialists should be involved with teacher and staff training and not with teaching youngsters in a remedial or developmental teaching situation (4). The responsibilities of these reading specialists should be quite broad. The office of the reading coordinator should assume major responsibility for the following four areas:

1. developing a districtwide reading program consistent with the direction of the board of education;
2. identifying appropriate materials and equipment needed to support the defined district reading program;
3. providing an adequate inservice training program for teachers, administrators, and aides; and
4. conducting an evaluation program that accurately determines the effectiveness of the reading program.

## Program Development

The reading coordinator shoulders the responsibility for producing, in writing, the goals of the district reading program. The goals and objectives of the reading program should not, however, be determined solely by the reading coordinator or any other individual. The coordinator bears the responsibility for translating into teachable reading objectives the philosophy of the community, as expressed through the board of education.

The reading coordinator should not determine the objectives of the district reading program without the broad involvement of others. He must encourage and actively solicit the involvement of teachers and administrators in the translation of general philosophy and direction to specific reading objectives.

Coordinating program development also carries the responsibility for identifying or developing the content of the program which will support the stated objectives. The coordinator is usually responsible for developing a curriculum guide to help teachers teach the objectives of the program.

Reading resource specialists usually assist the coordinator in all aspects of program development. They are often working members of curriculum development and writing committees; they spend less time in the planning phase of curriculum development and more time in the production and implementation phases.

## Identifying Materials to Support
## the Reading Program

Identifying instructional materials to support the objectives of the reading program is an extremely important function of the central office reading staff. Fewer school districts are pursuing a policy of single text adoption. The need to give teachers the option to choose from a wide variety of instructional materials is becoming more broadly accepted. As a result, the task of searching for and screening materials that will support the district reading goals is a time consuming and seemingly endless process. Currently, publishers are producing a deluge of materials for teaching reading. In order to avoid being inundated by sample reading materials, most central office personnel are spending disproportionate amounts of time screening and evaluating instructional materials.

## Providing Inservice Training

Many district reading personnel consider the task of providing effective inservice programs one of the most difficult responsibilities confronting them, often because of the constraints within the public school systems. Some of these constraints include holding inservice between 3:30 and 5:00 p.m. when teachers are tired or on Saturdays and evenings, often without additional pay for teachers; conducting inservice programs without an adequate budget to provide for multimedia materials to support the inservice presentations; or conducting inservice programs without the aid of outside consultants or specialists to help provide different approaches and fresh insights into inservice training.

In spite of these constraints, the responsibility for individualizing instruction does not rest alone with the classroom teacher. It seems a bit hypocritical to request that teachers work at individualizing instruction for children when the teachers of teachers often conduct inservice as if all teachers have the same needs. All the good reasons cited for individualizing instruction for children are just as valid for instructing adults.

Some of the findings reported by Durkin (2) strongly support the need to individualize teacher inservice training. Much inservice time is spent teaching teachers *how* to teach phonics—not considering whether teachers know the *content* of phonics. Durkin found that the teachers she studied did not really know phonics well enough to teach it. Effective inservice, like all effective teaching, hinges upon meeting individual needs. Persons who offer the same type of inservice training to all teachers, regardless of their needs, have rightfully earned the same criticism as teachers who teach all students the same material in the same way regardless of need and learning style.

Central office reading personnel need to be sensitive to how and when teachers learn best, how to arrange for effective group interaction, how to get willing participation in simulation experiences, how to present information effectively, and how to involve individuals actively when conducting inservice. The need to involve teachers in interesting, relevant inservice sessions warrants serious attention.

In the larger school districts, central office reading staffs are frequently faced with training large numbers of teachers, paraprofessionals, and administrators in new methods or new curriculum. The training demands on most central office personnel generally far exceed their abilities to meet these commitments. Perhaps the responsibility of training leadership in reading at the local building level should be included in the role of the central office reading staff. The local building resource person, if properly trained, can furnish much of the on-the-spot leadership that central office personnel often are not available to provide.

There is certainly no widespread agreement on how district level reading personnel should function in the school organization (3). There is considerable controversy about how to use these people most effectively. Some school districts will argue that central reading personnel should be "helpful friends" to teachers; that is, function in a staff position with no direct responsibility for holding teachers accountable for their performances as reading teachers. Other districts prefer to have central office reading personnel work in a line position; that is, be directly responsible for the quality of the teacher's reading instruction. The organizational pattern most widely used, however, places the reading coordinator or consultant in a staff position. In this organizational pattern the principal is directly responsible for the teacher's classroom performance. The central office reading staff offers support when needed and requested. The reading consultant is not an evaluator of the teacher's performance but is available to help if either the teacher or the principal believes that help is needed and requests it.

Being in an advisory capacity instead of a supervisory capacity brings about a climate more conducive to the building of a good working relationship between the central office staff and teachers. The services of the reading consultant are more apt to be requested if the teacher realizes that she can discuss her instructional problems and frustrations freely without fear of exposing weaknesses to the person responsible for rating her teaching performance and job efficiency.

Working in a staff relationship places the central office reading personnel in a somewhat odd position. The reading staff has the responsibility for developing a quality program, but it has no authority for seeing to it that the program is taught in accordance with the district policy or in accordance with the reading program as written. The responsibility for implementing the reading program falls to the building principal. It is entirely possible that a well-conceived and well-written reading program could fail because of the lack of strong leadership to implement the program at the local building level.

A major concern of the reading staff is to effect change in teacher behavior. It is entirely possible that the most effective tool for bringing about meaningful change in teaching behavior is the ability to work well with people. Change cannot be brought about effectively and lastingly by mandate—even by those who have the authority to issue mandates. Change therefore, must be brought about by means other than legislative change.

In order to work with people effectively and productively, central office reading personnel should have experience in group dynamics and human relations as part of their qualifications and preparations.

If working with people effectively is the most essential activity for bringing about change in teacher behavior, perhaps, one needs to reconsider what weighs most heavily in job interviews for central office reading personnel. Should it be great depth in reading course work or should it be evidence that the person being interviewed is "people centered" and understands how people learn most effectively?

## Evaluation

Too frequently the evaluation aspect of curriculum development is omitted entirely or treated too incidentally. Program evaluation must be an integral part of curriculum development. Program effectiveness must be monitored and evaluated continually.

A requisite of effective program evaluation is that the objectives of the reading program be clearly defined. Exactly what is the reading program trying to accomplish? It is the task of the central office reading staff to select the tests that best measure what the district reading program is trying to teach. Of course, this task might fall to a committee of teachers, parents, and others; but the ultimate responsibility for selecting the evaluation techniques or instruments should be the overall responsibility of the reading coordinator. If a standardized instrument is used, considerations need to be given to the reading skills evaluated by the test; the populations on which the test was normed; the norms provided (such as spring, fall, innercity); and the statistical information provided by the test scores. In this day of accountability and concern with cost effectiveness, evaluation cannot and should not be taken lightly.

## Summary

In summary, central office reading personnel are in a position to shape and to influence directly the district reading program. Their major responsibilities fall in the areas of 1) program development;

2) identification of materials to support the district program; 3) teacher, teacher aide, and administrator inservice (*1*); and 4) program evaluation.

All of these aspects of the job demand considerable planning and careful budgeting. Cost conscious communities, determined to get a dollar's worth of education for each dollar spent, are rightfully demanding a high level of efficiency from school personnel.

The changing nature of central office positions demands that persons hired for these positions have proficiencies far beyond just being a better than average reading teacher. Having experience as a successful reading teacher is most assuredly a necessary requisite for the job. Successful teaching experience alone, however, will not necessarily prepare a person adequately to organize materials, muster financial support, and direct human resources toward the successful development and implementation of a district reading program.

### References

1. Criscuolo, Nicholas P. "Approaches to Inservice Reading Programs," *Reading Teacher*, February 1971.

2. Durkin, Dolores. "Fundamental Principles Underlying Phonics Instruction," in Mildred Dawson (Compiler), *Teaching Word Recognition Skills*. Newark, Delaware: International Reading Association, 1971.

3. Morrill, Katherine A. "A Comparison of Two Methods of Reading Supervision," *Reading Teacher*, May 1966, 617.

4. Robinson, H. Alan, "The Reading Consultant of the Past, Present, and Possible Future," *Reading Teacher*, March 1967, 477.

5. "Roles, Responsibilities, and Qualifications of Reading Specialists," prepared by Professional Standards and Ethics Committee. Newark, Delaware: International Reading Association, 1968.

6. Smith, Nila B. *American Reading Instruction*. Newark, Delaware: International Reading Association, 1965.

# developing the reading program

"Yes, *two* of them—a *team* of teachers!"

# A CASE HISTORY APPROACH TO STUDY THE EFFECTS
# OF INDIVIDUALIZED READING INSTRUCTION

*Eunice N. Askov*
*University of Wisconsin*

Case histories of individual pupils were made to study the effects of
an individualized or "diagnostic teaching" approach to reading instruction—namely, the Wisconsin Design for Reading Skill Development. The purpose of the investigation was to determine what
adaptations for individual children were actually made with an individualized approach to instruction. The study was therefore considered exploratory in nature. Rather than comparing an experimental
school using the Design to a control school which was not using the
Design, the study was done only in a school where the Design had
been implemented and developed for several years to learn what
happened to individual children during reading instruction when the
Design was being systematically used.

Brief descriptions of the Design and of the school's organizational plan follow to provide a picture of the setting in which the
study took place.

## Wisconsin Design for Reading Skill Development

The purpose of the Design is to implement individually guided
education (IGE) in reading (3). In other words, each child's strengths
and weaknesses in reading skills are preassessed; then his instructional
program is designed to remedy problems with specific skills. Instruction takes place in groups of varying sizes. The distinguishing feature
of skill group instruction, which is part of the Design, is that all
children in a group lack the specific skill being taught and are ready
for instruction in it. However, there is also the recognition that
children may learn in different ways. Therefore, a variety of activities
and approaches is recommended during the course of instruction for
a given group.

As soon as a child gives evidence of having grasped the skill being
taught, he is dismissed from skill group instruction to work on

another skill need or to engage in independent activities. Thus, skill groups are flexible since frequent changes in composition are made to adjust for the changing needs of individual children.

Six areas of skill development are included in the Design. They are as follows: Word Attack, Comprehension, Study Skills, Self-Directed Reading, Interpretive Reading, and Creative Reading. Primary teachers in the school were encouraged to emphasize the word attack area as part of their work with the Research and Development Center. Furthermore, they were provided with more complete materials for assessing and teaching word attack skills than for the other skill areas.

The skills included in the Design are also grouped into five difficulty levels. The approximate grade equivalents for each level are as follows:

Level A—End of Kindergarten
Level B—End of Grade 1
Level C—End of Grade 2
Level D—End of Grade 3
Level E—Grades 4-6

A child should not necessarily be working on the skills at his grade level, however. Instead, he should be working on the skills at his instructional level, advancing to new skills as fast as his ability permits.

### Multiunit School

The case history study was done in a school which was organized into units rather than into grades. (A complete description of the multiunit organization can be found elsewhere (2).) Instead of self-contained classrooms, children are placed in a unit in which two grade levels are usually combined. Planning and instruction are done cooperatively by all the teachers in a unit rather than by each teacher alone for his classroom.

Children are placed in units by age rather than on the basis of achievement. A given child's instructional program, however, may be geared to a level other than the grade levels included in his unit. The grade equivalents for the various units in the school where the study was done are as follows:

Unit A: Kindergarten and Grade 1
Unit B: Grades 1 and 2
Unit C: Grades 2 and 3
Unit D: Grades 3 and 4
Unit E: Grades 5 and 6

The case history study was limited to students in grades 2-6 since the greatest impact of the Design usually occurs beyond the first grade level. Consequently, Unit A and the first graders in Unit B were not included in the study.

## Method

Teachers and aides were given only a minimal amount of the following information to insure that instruction would not be influenced by the gathering of case history data.

### Selection of Subjects and Observers

Three children beyond the first grade level in age were selected from each of the units. Within each unit, one child was selected randomly from the high IQ group, one from the average IQ group, and one from the low IQ group. Intelligence test scores—the most recent scores on the Lorge-Thorndike Intelligence Tests—were obtained from school records. The range of each group was as follows:

High IQ: 110-129

Average IQ: 90-109

Low IQ: 70-89

The clerical aide in each unit was selected as the most able to make unobtrusive observations of the children during reading instruction. Clerical aides do not participate in instruction and, therefore, their time is not rigidly structured. Although they know most of the children, the children do not look to them for help or instruction. Therefore, the clerical aides were free to enter classrooms to make observations without the disruption sometimes caused by observers who are not part of the school staff.

Within the time block set aside for reading instruction in each unit, the aide was assigned a different observation time for each day. They were, however, specifically instructed to observe skill instruction in reading whenever it was taking place, but to vary their observation times each day.

### Observation Instrument

The observation instrument was an adaptation of one used in a previous study (1). The observation form and accompanying instructions for its use are presented on pages 142-143.

Attempts were made to keep the form and instructions as simple and clear as possible to permit use by clerical aides. The aides were encouraged to ask teachers about the nature of the activities or skills if they were unsure how to mark the observation form. Questions about the use of the form were to be referred to the investigator.

## Training of the Observers

The investigator met with the clerical aides to explain their role in the study and to give them the observation form with the accompanying instructions on its use. Each item on the observation form was thoroughly discussed, and situations were simulated to provide practice for the aides in using the observation form. A pilot study was then run for ten days. At the completion of the pilot study, the investigator again met with the aides to determine what problems had been encountered, and the categories were further defined in light of observation experiences.

## Collection of Data

The clerical aides made one observation per day in each unit from early January through the end of March 1970—a total of ten weeks. Due to absences by children and by aides, the total number of observations collected varied within each unit and in no case equaled the total number of days that the study was in progress.

## Analyses, Results, and Conclusions

Since one type of analysis was performed on the data in several categories, the analyses, results, and conclusions are presented for these categories first: Activity, Group Size, Skill Area, Skill Level, and Modeling.

## Method of Analysis

The proportion of observations for each item within the categories of Activity, Group Size, Skill Area, Skill Level, and Modeling was computed. Then an estimate of the range of each proportion was calculated using the following probability statement:

$$\text{Probability } (\hat{p} - 2\sqrt{\frac{\hat{p}\hat{q}}{n}} \leq \hat{p} \leq \hat{p} + 2\sqrt{\frac{\hat{p}\hat{q}}{n}}) \approx .95$$

This probability statement assumes a normal distribution and uses the quantity $\sqrt{\frac{\hat{p}\hat{q}}{n}}$ as an estimation of the standard error of measurement.

The estimated ranges or intervals were used to compare 1) the proportions of time a particular unit or IQ group devoted to two or more activities (or other categories), and 2) the proportions of time two different units or IQ groups devoted to the same activity. The difference between two observed proportions was not considered statistically significant unless the corresponding interval estimates did not overlap.

## Results and Conclusions

*Activity*. When comparisons were made across units, certain types of activities predominated in particular units. Table 1 presents the estimated ranges for all the activity categories.

### TABLE 1

Range of Proportions of Activities for Units

| Type of Activity | Unit B | Unit C | Unit D | Unit E |
|---|---|---|---|---|
| Basal | .0617-.1673 | .0000* | .0540-.1596 | .0050-.0742 |
| Basal Workbook | .0188-.0880 | .0000 | .0504-.1480 | .0000 |
| Printed Programed Materials | .0210-.1010 | .0000 | .0000 | .0050-.0742 |
| Experience Charts | .0000 | .0000 | .0000 | .0000 |
| Board Work | .0428-.1404 | .2951-.4691* | .0428-.1404 | .0079-.0079* |
| Teacher-Made Materials | .0657-.1785 | .0912-.2176 | .1047-.2311 | .0749-.1949 |
| Commercial Reading Kits | .0617-.1673 | .0655-.1783 | .1093-.2417 | .0038-.0438* |
| Commercial Learning Kits | .0023-.0587* | .0000 | .0000 | .0000 |
| Audiovisual Materials | .0029-.0429 | .0141-.0833 | .0000* | .0464-.1440 |
| Supplementary Reading | .0393-.1285 | .0060-.0752 | .0317-.1209 | .1712-.3208* |
| Listening Activity | .0112-.0804 | .0000* | .0023-.0587 | .0385-.1361 |
| Other Language Arts Activity | .0112-.0804 | .0250-.1050 | .0926-.2126 | .1163-.2487 |
| Testing | .0029-.0429 | .0574-.1702 | .0188-.0880 | .0035-.0599 |
| Noninstructional Activity | .1246-.2570 | .0285-.1177 | .0112-.0804 | .0583-.1639 |

*The difference between this and other proportions in the same row can be considered statistically significant since the estimated ranges do not overlap.

The following conclusions may be drawn:

1. A variety of activities was observed in each unit. No unit concentrated even half of its time on one type of activity.

2. Some types of activities were infrequently observed. Experience charts, for example, were not seen at all. Basal workbooks and printed programed materials were not often observed, indicating that seatwork with commercial workbook materials was not a frequent activity in any unit. Testing was also not observed often. This finding is surprising in that skill tests are provided as part of the Design materials to preassess skill needs and to check skill attainment after instruction.

3. The use of different activities by older and younger children was generally as expected. For example, supplementary reading was observed significantly more often in Unit E than in other units. On the other hand, board work was found significantly most often in Unit C and least often in Unit E—a finding which is logical when one considers that the older children in Unit E frequently worked independently.

4. No significant differences were observed among units in the use of teacher-made materials. These were used more often than many other materials and activities by teachers in all units.

5. No differential treatment for ability levels was evident in terms of materials and activities. (These proportions, therefore, were not tabled.)

*Group size.* Comparisons made across units revealed some differences among units for each group size. The ranges are presented in Table 2.

### TABLE 2
Range of Proportions of Group Sizes for Units

| Group Size | Unit B | Unit C | Unit D | Unit E |
|---|---|---|---|---|
| Large | .0617-.1673 | .5146-.6886* | .0971-.2235 | .2802-.4498* |
| Medium | .1093-.2417* | .0043-.0443 | .4244-.5984* | .0050-.0742 |
| Small | .1246-.2570 | .0000-.0362 | .1369-.2753 | .0130-.0822 |
| One-to-one | .0029-.0429 | .0141-.0833 | .0428-.1404 | .0503-.1559 |
| Child Alone | .4091-.5831 | .2265-.3913 | .0023-.0587* | .3574-.5314 |

*The difference between this and other proportions in the same row can be considered statistically significant since the estimated ranges do not overlap.

The clearest way to present these findings is to show how each unit ranks in order of frequency for each group size (see Table 3). The assignment of different ranks indicates significant differences among the estimated intervals (i.e., the intervals do not overlap). On the other hand, when more than one unit is given the same rank, no significant differences exist among them.

### TABLE 3
Ranking of Units by Frequency of Observation for Each Group Size

| Large | Medium | Group Size Small | One-to-one | Child Alone |
|---|---|---|---|---|
| 1. Unit C | 1. Unit D | 1. Units D & B | n.s. | 1. Units B, E, & C |
| 2. Unit E | 2. Unit B | 2. Units E & C | | 2. Unit D |
| 3. Units D & B | 3. Units E & C | | | |

When comparisons were made across all units, no significant differences were found among the units in the use of one-to-one groupings. However, when Units B and E (the extremes in age groups) were compared, Unit E had significantly more one-to-one groupings. Large groups were observed most often in Unit C, medium in Unit D, and small in Units D and B. A child working alone was observed least often in Unit D.

The preference of teachers in each unit for particular types of groupings seems to indicate that once unit teachers decide on procedures for reading skill instruction, they tend to maintain the same procedures. This routine may be necessary to insure the smooth operation of instruction.

Similar comparisons were made across IQ groups. The estimated intervals are presented in Table 4. When the various group sizes were compared across the three IQ groups, significant differences were found only in the one-to-one grouping. Children of the low IQ group were included in this type of grouping significantly more often than children in the two other IQ groups. One would hope for this finding since the low IQ child probably needs more individual help and tutoring than children of the average and high IQ groups. However, in comparison to other group sizes, this grouping was not frequently observed in any IQ group although it was used more often with the low IQ children than with children of other ability levels.

When the average IQ group was omitted and only the high and low IQ groups were compared, it can be seen that the high IQ group was included in medium groupings significantly more often than the low IQ group. When only the average and the low IQ groups were compared, the low IQ group was observed significantly less often than the average IQ group in small groups. Thus, it appears that the low IQ children were given fewer opportunities to meet in small and medium groups than the two other IQ groups.

TABLE 4

Range of Proportions of Group
Sizes for IQ Groups and Total Group

| Group Size | High IQ | Average IQ | Low IQ | Total Group |
|---|---|---|---|---|
| Large | .1911-.3235 | .2447-.3831 | .2732-.4172 | .2652-.3452 |
| Medium | .1852-.3176 | .1318-.2518 | .0821-.1797 | .1571-.2263 |
| Small | .0606-.1498 | .1180-.2308 | .0368-.1060 | .0892-.1456 |
| One-to-one | .0025-.0375 | .0241-.0805 | .0821-.1797* | .0465-.0865 |
| Child Alone | .2964-.4404 | .2012-.3336 | .2522-.3906 | .2789-.3589 |

*The difference between this and other proportions in the same row can be considered statistically significant since the estimated ranges do not overlap.

Comparisons of different group sizes within each IQ group and within the total group may also be made from Table 4 by reading down the columns. The ranking orderings are presented in Table 5.

Within the total group of subjects, children were observed working alone and in large groups most frequently. The other group sizes observed—in order of frequency of observation—were medium, small, and one-to-one groupings.

TABLE 5

Ranking of Group Sizes by Frequency of Observation
within Each IQ Group and within the Total Group

| High IQ | Average IQ | Low IQ | Total Group |
|---|---|---|---|
| 1. Child Alone, Large, and Medium Groups | 1. Large, Child Alone, Medium, and Small Groups | 1. Large and Child Alone Groups | 1. Child Alone and Large Groups |
| 2. Small Groups | 2. One-to-one | 2. Medium, One-to-one, and Small Groups | 2. Medium Group |
| 3. One-to-one | | | 3. Small Group |
| | | | 4. One-to-one |

With the use of the Design one would expect more frequent use of small and medium groupings for specific skill instruction than was observed since individualization can be achieved through groups which meet each child's needs rather than necessarily through provision of individual instruction. The frequent observation of a child working alone, however, may be an artifact of the observational system. Aides were instructed to mark the observation form as "child alone" if the child were doing independent work even while in a group setting. Thus, he might have been part of a group even though he was doing independent work at the time he was observed. Although independent work might indeed be part of group instruction, the observation was classified as "child alone" to keep the observational system straightforward. Thus, participation in a group was marked only when the child was actively engaged in group work—not when he was working independently in a group setting.

*Skill area.* The ranges of the proportions across and within units were not tabled for skill areas since many of the cells were empty. The word attack area was taught more than other areas in all units except Unit E where both word attack and comprehension skills predominated over other areas. The emphasis on the word attack area was probably due to the nature of the work being done in cooperation with the Research and Development Center.

The estimated intervals for the various areas within each IQ group were not tabled since no significant differences among IQ groups were found. Again, the word attack area predominated.

*Skill level.* Table 6 presents the estimated intervals for the four difficulty levels across units. Table 7 presents a rank ordering of each level across units. Table 8 shows the rank ordering of different levels within each unit and within the total group.

## TABLE 6

Range of Proportions of Skill Levels for Units

| Level | Unit B | Unit C | Unit D | Unit E |
|-------|--------|--------|--------|--------|
| B | 1.0000* | .6322-.8110* | .1563-.3859* | .0000-.1386* |
| C | .0000* | .1889-.3677 | .5563-.7995* | .0479-.2631 |
| D | .0000 | .0000 | .0000-.1072 | .5771-.8451* |
| E | .0000 | .0000 | .0000 | .0000-.1386 |

*The difference between this and other proportions in the same row can be considered statistically significant since the estimated ranges do not overlap.

## TABLE 7

Ranking of Units by Frequency
of Observation for Each Skill Level

| Level B | Level C | Level D | Level E |
|---------|---------|---------|---------|
| 1. Unit B | 1. Unit D | 1. Unit E | n.s. |
| 2. Unit C | 2. Units C and E | 2. Unit D | |
| 3. Unit D | | | |
| 4. Unit E | | | |

## TABLE 8

Ranking of Skill Levels by Frequency of Observation
for Each Unit and for the Total Group

| Unit B | Unit C | Unit D | Unit E | Total Group |
|--------|--------|--------|--------|-------------|
| 1. Level B | 1. Level B | 1. Level C | 1. Level D | 1. Level B |
| | 2. Level C | 2. Level B | 2. Levels C, B, and E | 2. Level C |
| | | 3. Level D | | 3. Level D |
| | | | | 4. Level E |

It can be noted from Table 7 that Level B was used significantly most often in Unit B, followed by Unit C. Level C skills were taught significantly most often in Unit D, and Level D skills in Unit E.

Even when the total group of subjects was considered, Level B was still the most frequently taught level, followed in frequency by Levels C, D, and E. Undoubtedly, teachers were providing instruction in the more elementary word attack skills. One must wonder, however, whether the children who were functioning at and above grade level in reading were receiving the correct levels of instruction.

When difficulty levels were considered across IQ groups, no

significant differences were found among the groups. (This information, therefore, was not tabled.) In other words, not even the children of high ability were working at significantly different difficulty levels from the low IQ children. Again, one must question the amount of individualization provided for children of high ability.

*Modeling.* As a type of one-to-one grouping, modeling may occur when one child serves as a model for another child as he helps him in instruction. Table 9 presents the estimated intervals for modeling in units and Table 10 shows the use of modeling in the IQ groups.

TABLE 9

Range of Proportions of Modeling for Units

| Modeling | Unit B | Unit C | Unit D | Unit E |
|---|---|---|---|---|
| Had model | .0000-.8773 | .5295-1.0000 | 1.0000 | .0000 |
| Was model | .1226-1.0000 | .0000-.4704 | .0000 | 1.0000 |

TABLE 10

Range of Proportions of Modeling for IQ Groups

| Modeling | High IQ | Average IQ | Low IQ |
|---|---|---|---|
| Had model | .0000* | .3174-1.0000 | .4561-.9189 |
| Was model | 1.0000* | .0000-.6826 | .0811-.5439 |

*The difference between this and other proportions in the same row can be considered statistically significant since the estimated ranges do not overlap.

When comparisons were made across units, it can be seen that in no one unit did the child being observed have a model significantly more often than in all other units. However, it can be noted that children in Unit E served as models for other children significantly more often than in Units C and D.

Comparing across IQ groups, the child being observed had a model significantly least often if he was of the high IQ group. He was also most likely to be a model if he was of the high IQ group. In fact, all of the times a high IQ child was observed in modeling situations, he was serving as a model for another child.

Data from these two other categories were also studied: Extent of Skill Group Instruction and Number of Teachers.

## Method of Analysis

The number of times that groups met for skill instruction was studied in relation to the number of skills that were taught. A ratio was created by dividing the number of group meetings by the number of skills. This ratio represented the average number of sessions devoted to testing or teaching each skill. An observation of a group meeting was not counted as a skill group session unless it was specifically indicated as such on the observation form.

The number of different teachers instructing each child was computed by dividing the number of different teachers' or aides' names listed on the observation forms in a given unit or IQ group by the number of children in that group.

### Results and Conclusions

*Extent of skill group instruction.* The frequencies of meetings of skill groups and the number of different skills that were being tested and taught are presented in Table 11.

TABLE 11
Extent of Skill Group Instruction

| | Number of Skill Group Meetings | Number of Different Skills Taught | Meetings / Skills |
|---|---|---|---|
| **Units** | | | |
| B | 34 | 11 | 3.09 |
| C | 94 | 20 | 4.70 |
| D | 50 | 15 | 3.33 |
| E | 42 | 26 | 1.62 |
| **IQ Groups** | | | |
| High | 71 | 21 | 3.38 |
| Average | 81 | 27 | 3.00 |
| Low | 68 | 24 | 2.83 |
| **Total Group** | 220 | 72 | 3.06 |

It appears that the greatest amount of instruction per skill was provided in Unit C and the least amount in Unit E. This finding in Unit E is perhaps an indication that older children needed only a review of skills rather than intensive work on developing new skills. The ratios for the three IQ groups were similar to each other and to that of the total group.

*Number of teachers.* The average number of different teachers that each child had ranged from 2.67 in Unit D to 4.00 in Unit C. This range reflected the methods of handling instruction in a multi-unit school where teachers were encouraged to teach the skills in which they felt most knowledgable rather than necessarily teaching the same group of children. The average number of teachers instructing each child in the various IQ groups was similar to that of the total group—3.33.

## Discussion

Techniques of classroom observation and data analysis proved to be workable in gathering information about an individual's learning situations. Given a well-defined observation form and training in its use, clerical aides were able to make unobtrusive and accurate classroom observations. Evidence of individualization of reading instruction was apparent, especially in the development and reinforcement of the more elementary skills. Anticipated differences among age groups were also found; however, adaptations for ability level did not appear to be made as frequently as adjustments for age. The conclusion was thus drawn that teachers were individualizing reading instruction in elementary skills for students of low and average abilities. However, provisions for developing higher level skills in bright students were generally not made.

To check the validity of the case history findings, the unit leaders in the school were asked to read a report of the study and to make comments. In general, they agreed with the findings, particularly noting that individualization of instruction for the high IQ children was lacking at the time of the study. The only finding they took issue with was the relatively small amount of testing observed. Two explanations seem plausible in accounting for this discrepancy: 1) The aides may not have recognized a testing situation and marked it as skill instruction. 2) Teachers may have been doing much testing in comparison with that of previous years but in fact doing a small amount when compared with the time spent on other activities during reading instruction.

This type of study provided important descriptive data that are often overlooked in assessing the effects of a reading program. By randomly choosing a limited number of students for observation, information about the daily operation of reading instruction in the classroom can be obtained. In addition, valuable feedback can be provided to the teaching staff, giving them an objective perspective of reading instruction in their school.

This study was also unique in the use of school personnel to make classroom observations. Contamination of the data due to an "experimenter effect" was thus avoided. The techniques employed in this study could be used by a school staff to study their own reading program or by researchers to monitor the daily operation of an experimental reading program in a school.

# References

1. Askov, Eunice Nicholson. *Assessment of a System for Individualizing Reading Instruction.* Technical Report No. 117. Madison: Wisconsin Research and Development Center for Cognitive Learning, 1970.

2. Klausmeier, Herbert J., et al. *Individually Guided Education in the Multiunit Elementary School: Guidelines for Implementation.* Madison: Wisconsin Research and Development Center for Cognitive Learning, 1968.

3. Otto, Wayne, and Eunice Askov. *Wisconsin Design for Reading Skill Development: Rationale and Guidelines.* Minneapolis, Minnesota: National Computer Systems, 1970.

## Observation Form

NAME_____ UNIT_____ DATE _____

### List Information under Size of Group

| | Large (16+) | Medium (8-15) | Small (2-7) | One-to-one (Child with Teacher, Aide, or Older Child) | Child Alone |
|---|---|---|---|---|---|
| Activitiy (check) Basal Basal Workbook Printed Programed Materials Experience Charts Board Work Teacher-Made Materials (including games) Commercial Reading Kits (including games) Commercial Learning Kits (including games) Audiovisual Materials Supplementary Reading Listening Activity Other Language Arts Activity Testing Noninstructional Activity | | | | | |
| Skill on Design Outline (name, if applicable) | | | | | |
| Teacher's or Aide's Name, if applicable | | | | | |
| No. of Boys in Group, if applicable | | | | | |
| No. of Girls in Group, if applicable | | | | | |
| Location (classrooms, learning center, library, etc.) | | | | | |

## Instructions for Using Observation Forms

1. Observe each of the three children in your unit at the specified time each day:
   Monday
   Tuesday
   Wednesday
   Thursday
   Friday

2. Do not call attention to yourself as you enter the classroom, learning center, etc. If possible, observe from the sidelines what each of the three children are doing. Do not ask the child what he is doing. If you have a question about what the activity is, ask the teacher or instructional aide when he is free.

3. Mark the items in the left column (i.e., Activity, Skill, Teacher's Name, Number of Boys, and Number of Girls) under the appropriate vertical column. For example, if a child is using a basal in a medium-sized group, you would place a check mark in the Medium column across from the word Basal. The Skill, Teacher's Name, etc. would also be marked in the column labeled Medium.

4. Definition of items in left column:

   Activity

   *Basal.* Basic reading book used for reading instruction.

   *Basal Workbook.* Workbook (usually a paperback in which a child writes his answers) that accompanies basal reader.

   *Printed Programed Materials.* Reading materials with a programed format.

   *Experience Charts.* Activity during which the child (individually or in a group) tells a story to an adult who writes it down for the child to read.

   *Board Work.* Instruction that uses the chalk board as the only medium of instruction. The child may be at the board or listening to the teacher who is using the chalk board in teaching.

   *Teacher-Made Materials.* Games, worksheets, activities, etc. constructed by the teacher or aide.

   *Commercial Reading Kits.* Commercial games, workbooks, worksheets, etc. that do *not* accompany the basal series, but that are used as supplementary material in reading instruction.

   *Commercial Learning Kits.* Commercial games, workbooks, worksheets, etc. that do *not* teach reading skills as such. Include here Frostig materials, Peabody Language Kit, Ginn Language Kit, etc.

   *Audiovisual Materials.* Work using an overhead projector, film, filmstrip, tape recorder, etc.

   *Supplementary Reading.* Magazines, literary readers, library books, etc. that are *not* part of the basal reading program.

   *Listening Activity.* Listening to a story, participating in a discussion, receiving training in hearing sounds, etc.

   *Other Language Arts Activity.* Spelling, handwriting, speaking, etc.

   *Testing.* Standardized, commercial, teacher-made, or informal tests and quizzes.

   *Noninstructional Activity.* Discipline problem, changing activities, or listening to procedures for upcoming activities.

   Skill on Design Outline. Name, level, and number of skill being taught if the activity is directed toward developing a skill on the Design outline. It probably would be necessary to ask the teacher or instructional aide for this information.

   Teacher's or Aide's Name. Name of teacher or aide if the child is directly involved in work with an adult. If the child is working with an older child, write in *older child*. If the child is doing independent work with a teacher or aide only as a resource person to answer questions, leave this row blank.

   Number of Boys in Group. Number of boys other than the child being observed. If the child is doing independent work (even though other children are present, but not directly working with the child), leave this row blank.

   Number of Girls in Group. Same as category above.

   Location. Place where instruction is taking place (classroom, learning center, library, etc.).

# READING IS FUNDAMENTAL

*Margaret McNamara*
*Reading is Fundamental*
*Washington, D.C.*

The aims of the International Reading Association (IRA) and of Reading Is Fundamental (RIF) are identical: encouraging children to read. IRA concerns involve development of teaching techniques. RIF does not teach, it motivates; and we know that where there is motivation, the job is easier.

This paper does not reveal some new, startling method of teaching reading; nor does it present a dazzling, visionary, grandiose program costing millions. Quite the contrary, it presents a modest, local experiment that is growing into a broad national program. It is based on some old and obvious truths and on some basic, immutable human motivations. And, relatively speaking, the costs are very low. They actually come down to two and one-half books for one dollar—but let us begin at the beginning.

Reading Is Fundamental began as a result of volunteer work in a reading program for black children in innercity Washington in 1966. It happened one day as I was reading with David from a book that had belonged to one of my own children. I offered the youngster the book—his to keep. His eyes opened wide; he could not believe he could actually *own* the book, and it took some persuasion on my part to convince him that I was really giving it to him.

It was then that the obvious struck me. Of course; books in my home are so taken for granted, so much a way of life, that it never occurred to me that poor children do not have books of their own. The poor not only lack the usual fare—Grimm's, King Arthur, the Bobbsey Twins—they have *no* reading matter, certainly none that relates to their own, everyday lives. If you carry that a short step beyond, you realize that their parents have no books either and frequently are no more literate than their children. This disadvantage is an end product of poverty, along with malnutrition, poor vision, inattention in class, disinterest, and, worst of all, the psychic wounds that breed cynics at a very young age.

I talked with Kay Lumley and others about this problem, and we decided we would create an experimental group in the capital; we would try to provide relevant books to poor children. We would buy paperback books suitable for children ranging from first to sixth grades, relevant books if we could find them. We would permit the children to choose any book at all from our stock—no restrictions of any kind, absolute freedom of choice for them. And once the child selected his book, it was his to keep. It worked very well, indeed. But even today, as we work with black children, Indian children, and Spanish-speaking children, we find that at our first distribution the child finds it hard to believe that this book, chosen by him, really does belong to him.

From that small experiment, which was funded by the Ford Foundation and sponsored by the Smithsonian Institution, we have grown and we are growing.

Although our concentration has been primarily in urban centers, we do have a project on the Indian reservation near Flagstaff, Arizona. We have one beginning with Chicano children in East Los Angeles and hope to have another Spanish-speaking project in Albuquerque. We have two rural projects: one based in Jackson, Mississippi, and another in Huntington, West Virginia. Other projects are based in Cleveland, Ohio; Centreville, Maryland; Columbus, Indiana; Philadelphia and Pittsburgh, Pennsylvania; St. Louis, Missouri; and Washington, D.C. The American Association of University Women has started a RIF program in Racine, Wisconsin. In Syracuse, New York, a woman has secured enough Title I funds to start a RIF program for twenty-six public and parochial schools.

We are helping to set up a RIF project for the children of migrant workers in Florida, sponsored by the Coca-Cola Company. A large New York utility has asked us for a proposal. A group of bankers and civic leaders in Chicago want us to tell them how to get a RIF program going in that city. We have received grants from Continental Oil, Gulf Oil, IBM, and others. As you can see, our sponsors, our underwriters, are many and varied. We aren't choosy. We work with almost anyone and everyone to get books into the hands of children.

A simple idea like RIF, and it is simple and obvious, is not always easy to put across. Many of us have grown so accustomed to thinking in what I call the Washington Syndrome—the big picture, the vast program, the billions of dollars—that thinking down to a mere five books a year per child gives some of us the mental bends. When we consider that those five books per child may cost as little as two dollars, our thinking must be readjusted. But, I am getting ahead of my story.

What will interest IRA is the business of books, the business of reading. What books really interest children? To what books can an Indian child on a reservation, a Chicano or a black child in the innercity of a metropolis relate? Well, you can bet that books about Sue and Tom who go on a camping trip and ride the rapids with Mommy and Daddy won't qualify. Some children may spend their vacation that way; but to a poor child, shooting the rapids is as remote as going to the moon, perhaps more remote to today's TV watchers.

The essence of RIF is to give the children books on subjects they know about or want to know about, names they recognize, and history they identify with. Don't offer *Black Beauty*, for instance. Most black children would be astonished to find it is about a horse.

We select RIF books with great care. The number of titles is limited; but since we began in 1966, the list has grown considerably. And we have put together a book list that is relevant. Books for Spanish-speaking and Indian children are particularly difficult to find, but we do have some. The list includes biographies, folklore, fiction, history of Indian heroes; the same is true in the Spanish-speaking category and for black children. The books relate to today, now, or to the history the children could have played a part in. For preschoolers and the lower elementary grades there are ABCs, arithmetic books, puzzles, jokes, and animal stories.

The books are inexpensive but attractive paperbacks and they come from a variety of publishers. We are working hard to persuade publishers that hardcover books costing $3.95 or more, relevant or not, will have a small market among poor people. These same poor would probably buy books produced in fifty cent paperback editions. We are now creating a market for the inexpensive paperback; we hope that publishers and distributors will return the compliment by printing the books and getting them into the communities where they will sell.

That is a peripheral problem. Our primary goal right now is to establish more and more RIF projects, order the books in bulk at wholesale prices, and get them to the children anyway we can.

Our books are so popular that teachers are stealing them. A harsh word, but true, for the teachers are as eager as we to get their hands on books to which pupils will respond. "Where do you find these books?" they ask us. "Where can we get them?"

We have learned a lot these past few years, a number of lessons as obvious and as simple as RIF itself; namely:

- If a book is labeled "Easy to Read," no child will touch it. It's a matter of pride, and he will not carry a book that puts him down.

- The younger the child, the more responsive he is. By the time a child reaches the fifth or sixth grade, he can be very suspicious.

- Freedom of choice is absolutely essential for a successful program. We know. A child is put off when a teacher or other adult discourages him from taking the book of his choice and tries to foist another on him. He may take the teacher's choice, but he is unlikely to read it.

- RIF books are precious objects. Many teachers and principals have told us that although they see some textbooks left behind in classrooms, cafeteria, on steps, or in corridors, RIF books are rarely left behind carelessly.

- RIF books are private, personal property. They are taken home, shared with brothers and sisters, read by parents, jealously guarded. One little boy says he has asked his mother to keep his books in her locked cupboard so that the books will not be mishandled by his two-year-old sister. The pride of ownership is the key.

- Books are becoming a part of the children's lives. Some children have started their own libraries in order to exchange books with one another. Children are sharing in classes, in community centers, in churches—wherever there are RIF distributions.

- But the proof that RIF works was revealed in the statement of a Pittsburgh teacher who reported that in the first few months after RIF started, school library circulation doubled!

Thus far, in all its projects, RIF has distributed 1.5 million books to about 275,000 children.

I hope that readers become motivated to start RIF projects in their own areas. Anyone can do it. It is not difficult. At RIF headquarters in Washington, we can provide technical assistance, and workshops if necessary, to show you how it is done. It is important to remember that all local RIF projects must be self-supporting; so the money for books and administrative costs, if there are any, must be borne by your locality. In some instances, Title I funds are available where schools will cooperate; in others, foundations help. Business corporations can be donors, or the PTA, or the local bank, or other organizations.

I need not tell you that all the teaching in the world, all the latest techniques and programs and machines and devices, will not work unless a child *wants* to read, unless he is motivated somehow to learn. It is up to us to motivate children. If we don't, they will not learn; their futures will be limited, unrewarding, bleak. And then, so will ours.

# LITERARY EXPERIENCES FOR TODAY'S CHILDREN

*Jean M. LePere*
*Michigan State University*

Adults who are concerned with the education of young children in a society which is becoming increasingly more mechanized and computerized may find themselves faced almost daily with new frustrations when seeking to guide the learning experiences of children. Every year countless new systems for the teaching of reading are to be found in the marketplace. As teachers, parents, reading specialists, and others attempt to evaluate the myriad materials that are available, it is entirely possible to lose sight of what ought to be the fundamental objectives of a sound instructional reading program for elementary school children.

What is the purpose of teaching reading in the elementary school? What are some justifiable objectives for teaching children to read in a society which has provided television and a host of other media for the purposes of entertainment and the dissemination of information? Indeed, can the teaching of reading still be justified in such a society? Is there still a need for the learner to read?

"Of course," most teachers and parents will readily respond, "It is imperative that the individual be able to read in order to function effectively in a literate society."

## The Objectives of a Sound Instructional
## Reading Program

Few would argue, therefore, that it is important to teach children to read. And further, most people will agree that one of the major objectives of the elementary school program is to turn out children who are *good* readers. But what is a good reader? Usual responses to that question may be that the reader "understands what is read," "reads well at his level" (whatever that means), or "can read well independently."

All of these definitions of a good reader call for closer examination and for a great deal of explanation. A sound program of reading instruction should provide the learner with materials and experiences which will assist him in developing certain skills as a responsible and efficient reader. Among such objectives, which have as their overarching purpose the development of good readers, might be those which seek to ensure that the learner develop 1) skills that will enable him to read well independently, 2) an ever-broadening interest in reading, 3) an appreciation and understanding of how language is used to communicate effectively, 4) an appreciation for the components of literature, and 5) an ability to respond critically and responsibly to printed matter.

Objectives, however, are frequently easily stated but far more difficult to achieve. As one observes practices in the teaching of reading in classrooms throughout the country, it is obvious that all schools do concentrate in one way or another on the task of teaching skills which are designed to enable the learner to read well independently. But when emphasis is placed upon skills with the exclusion of interest and appreciation, the result is that children frequently find reading a troublesome chore.

Appreciation skills, however, are somewhat difficult to teach; and, at best, the evaluation process for determining one's level of appreciation and ability to read critically is elusive. Thus, it can be observed that many young learners still do not achieve the objectives related to enjoyment, appreciation, and critical response to printed matter.

## The Content of the Instructional Reading Program

If the major objectives of teaching children to read are that they read well independently, enjoy reading, appreciate what is read, and respond critically, then one is led to the fairly simple conclusion that the content of what a child reads ought to be exciting and interesting. With the abundance of sensitively written and beautifully illustrated trade books available in children's libraries, it should not be difficult to locate such material. Frequently, however, the literature or library program is viewed as separate from the instructional reading program with the result that at times an inordinate amount of time is spent in drilling the mechanical skills of reading while little time is left for engaging in activities which are designed to achieve goals connected with enjoyment and appreciation.

Such a state of affairs need not exist. It is proposed that a sound program of literary appreciation can be interwoven with a sound basal instructional reading program. The two should not be viewed as separate entities but rather as integral components of the same instructional undertaking.

### Literary Experiences for Children:
### Points of View

Varying points of view may be identified with reference to what ought to constitute literary experiences for children during the elementary school years. Such viewpoints range from those held by individuals who would contend that instruction during the elementary school years should focus upon objectives related to the development of reading skills and simple enjoyment with little attention to appreciation and critical reading to those who would support a strong and developmental literature program throughout the child's school experience.

Cullinan (1) identifies such points of view as those ranging from opposition to a literature program to those which view teaching literature as a planned program for which the main objectives are the enjoyment of literature and a continued interest in reading. Recommendations emerging from the 1968 Dartmouth University Anglo-American Seminar in the Teaching of English support the point of view that, while literature should have a place in the elementary school, such a program should be informal until grades five or six (4).

A survey by Odland (3) indicates that current approaches to the teaching of literature in the elementary school fall roughly into four categories: 1) teaching literature as a subject, with methods similar to secondary schools and colleges; 2) a library period with guidance from the librarian; 3) a planned literature program with the main objective being enjoyment of literature and continued interest in reading; and 4) using literature as a secondary goal in the teaching and learning process, where objectives are only indirectly related to literature.

Similar differences in points of view may be cited with reference to the teaching of literary criticism and critical reading at the elementary school level. The purpose of this presentation is not to debate the points of view but rather to suggest what is deemed to be a feasible and sensible plan for involving children in literary experiences in the developmental reading program which will assist them in achieving the objectives of interest, appreciation, and critical response.

### Evaluative and Creative Response to Reading Matter

From his very first experience in reading, a child ought not to be denied the opportunity to read material which is interesting to him and in which he can find some opportunity for personal relationship.

This point of view implies that the focus of instruction should go beyond the mastery of mechanical skills and literal comprehension to give the learner opportunity to evaluate what has been read and to make personal application of the printed context. In 1958, Eller (2) noted that:

> ... A reader who has mastered the reading mechanics and who comprehends literally without attempting to evaluate the printed context is in possession of a dangerous weapon. He is just as well equipped to become misinformed through reading as to become enlightened.

The relevance of what the printed word brings to the reader lies in his ability to react in an evaluative and creative manner. If children are expected to so react, they need to have experiences with reading material which is representative of various types of literature. From their earliest reading experiences, children need opportunities to be engaged in activities which call for literal responses to content and also interpretive and evaluative reactions. Enjoyment of reading can be enhanced through meaningful discussion which calls upon the learner to think about what has been read. Observation and practice have proven that very young children are capable of such thinking.

The literal question simply asks the reader to recall what he has read. While this may be a very important step for the beginning reader (for example, the reconstruction of the sequence of events in a story), a much higher level of thinking is called for when one is asked to interpret what has been read. Here the individual reacts to certain facets of a selection in terms of his own life experiences, or he may attempt to more fully understand language usage. At the third level, that of evaluation or critical response, the learner must bring his own value system into play, and it is through such thinking that he is able to build a value system of his own. When he responds to reading matter in an evaluative manner, he must justify his conclusion and build a defense for his response. As the child matures, he needs to be helped to discover that he must develop a logical rationale to defend his conclusions.

## Experiences with Literature

If children are expected to respond in interpretive and creative ways, then they must have material made available to them which lends itself to such response. When it is suggested that trade books be included in the instructional reading program, many teachers feel that developmental skills of reading may be overlooked. There is no reason why children cannot read widely under the guidance of the teacher and at the same time acquire the necessary skills to become independent readers.

For years a common complaint has been that the content of the basal reader was not challenging, was boring, or was irrelevant to the children who read it. A careful analysis of the content of contemporary, reputable basal readers reveals that authors and publishers have made a sincere effort to provide balance in types of literature represented, ethnic and regional selections, and representations of outstanding literature for children. Thus, the total blame for unchallenging content can no longer be placed on the basal readers if selections are made wisely and professionally.

But no basal reading program purports to give the learner all of the experiences he should have with literature in order to become a mature and critical reader. There is no reason why a child cannot begin to read trade books almost immediately after formal instruction in reading is begun, if the instruction in reading is soundly based upon the objectives outlined.

The beginning reader can read some realistic stories, such as those written by Ezra Jack Keats, Charlotte Zolotow, Lois Lenski, or Helen Buckley. There will be some simple animal stories that many children can handle, such as *The Biggest Bear, Make Way for Ducklings*, and *April's Kittens*. At this level the reading will be primarily for enjoyment and perhaps for some personal identification. The teacher will do much reading aloud to the children, also. There will be no attempt at literary classification, but discussions will call for some simple interpretations and evaluations. Poetry will be enjoyed as it is read by the teacher. In this way the young child will be led to discover gradually that poetry deals with words and rhythm in language. He will be exposed to poetry which deals with concepts, but never will the poetry be so abstract that he is unable to relate it to the world of which he is a part. Critical thinking may be stimulated through sharing concept books, such as *A Tree is Nice* or *The Important Book*.

Very soon the child should be helped to distinguish between forms of literature which represent the real world and those which represent the world of make-believe. The six-year-old can make gross distinctions between stories which tell about things which really could happen to anyone who lives in his world and those in which animals talk or imaginary personages such as fairies and giants appear.

At succeeding levels of maturity, children can be helped to discover the significance of the components of literature. Seven- and eight-year-olds can distinguish elements of setting which relate to time and location. Even though time and distance concepts are difficult for the very young child to understand, he can draw gross conclusions as to whether a story might have taken place a long time ago or could be happening in the world in which he lives.

Forms of literature can be gradually conceptualized by the child as he learns that some stories are called folktales and as he learns to understand their nature.

Purely informational material will comprise another dimension of the reading diet of the individual as he matures in his ability to read a variety of materials and to distinguish among forms of written material. Eight- and nine-year-olds can be helped to discover that biographies are stories which tell about the lives of real people. Other material provides information about the world around us and provides an opportunity to respond in an evaluative manner to determine the objectivity of the presentation of the material.

The important point is that the literature program ought not to be viewed as separate from the reading program. What does one read as he goes through life? He reads fiction, fantasy, biography, informational materials, poetry—all forms of literature. Instruction in reading ought to be so designed that the learner reads literature as a part of the instructional process. A sound instructional program in reading should concern itself with assisting children to master the skills of word analysis which will enable them to become independent in attacking vocabulary as new materials are encountered. But the teaching of reading is much more than this; it should provide children with opportunity to understand and appreciate the components of literature: setting, theme, plot, characters, and literary style. It should help children to recognize and appreciate forms of literature: fiction (realism, fantasy), folk literature, poetry, biography, and information. It should, above all, provide planned and sequential activities for critical response to what has been read.

A sound reading program which incorporates much literature will have as its prime objective the enjoyment and satisfaction that the reader gains from his reading experience. Literature will not be viewed as distinct from the reading program; it will be an integral part of the program and will provide the materials for reading instruction. Library periods will not be once-a-week occurrences; rather, the daily experiences in reading will embrace a wide variety of literary materials. The program will be planned with a sound knowledge of basic developmental characteristics and interests of children in mind, coupled with professional knowledge of the wealth of materials which are available in the trade books for children.

Children in the elementary school years are capable of responding to what they have read in interpretive and evaluative ways. An instructional reading program which fails to take this matter into consideration is deemed inadequate. In order to help children to enjoy reading, to build an ever-increasing enthusiasm for reading, and to become responsible and mature critical readers, the instructional program must provide opportunities for extensive exposure to all forms of literature and embody instructional techniques which are designed to help the learner to relate the matter which he has read to his own life in a meaningful and evaluative way.

### References

1. Cullinan, Bernice E. *Literature for Children: Its Discipline and Content.* Dubuque, Iowa: William C. Brown Company, 1971, 86-89.

2. Eller, William. "Fundamentals of Critical Reading," *The Reading Teacher's Reader.* New York: Ronald Press, 1958, 30-34.

3. Odland, Norine. *Teaching Literature in the Elementary School.* Champaign, Illinois: National Council of Teachers of English, 1969.

4. Squire, James R. (Ed.). *Response to Literature.* Champaign, Illinois: National Council of Teachers of English, 1968.

# THE ONTOGENY OF READING

*Nicholas A. Glaser*
*University of Northern Colorado*

The volume of research focusing on reading instruction increases dramatically each year. Yet, it would appear that in seeking answers through quality research more questions than solutions are created; perhaps this result is to be expected as a natural concomitant of the research process. So be it, but the teachers who are the key to success in a reading program are the ones who must sift out—often with little help—the pragmatic ideas and direction from the plethora of suggestions flooding the reading scene. Sometimes sociologists, psychologists, neurologists, and linguists seem to be more concerned with reading than the reading educators themselves. In fact, in many instances, the point of view of the reading educator seems to be influenced more by those outside his area of specialization than by those within. In some instances, the multidisciplinary involvement has contributed to polarization and confusion rather than aiding the teacher in consolidating her beliefs in a meaningful manner.

The purpose of this article is to illustrate the dilemma the classroom teacher faces as he attempts to evaluate critically the rapidly accumulating research and the resulting opinions which emanate from interpretation of the results. To accomplish this purpose, it seems that it would be most effective to use the familiar breakdown outlining the developmental nature of the basic skills of reading. The concern will be with the origin and development of reading within the educational setting where the skill is learned or "taught." Hence, the skill areas included will be readiness, picture cues, contextual cues, word identification, and comprehension.

This particular emphasis has been taken because a generalization which can be made with a certain amount of confidence is that the teacher makes the difference in the establishment and implementation of a successful reading program. The teacher is in need of guidance and direction as he makes decisions which breathe life into a reading program and which start a student on his way to learning to read. Where does the teacher find this assistance? Research, experts, conferences, and many other sources are available, but what have they really provided?

## Readiness

Most authorities would agree that the child comes to school with considerable facility for spoken language. As Gibson (7) states:

> The child has learned to segment a sequential stream of acoustic information; to divide it into useful units of structure; to discriminate these units by means of an economical set of distinctive features; to assign symbolic meanings to units of an appropriate size; to infer rules that structure the unit in permissible ways; and even to recombine these units in rulelike ways so as to produce original messages.

The teacher's task is to help the child bridge the gap between his oral language and a strange new medium that he is told represents his spoken words. It appears that linguists are underestimating reading teachers when they suggest that they depart from tradition by recognizing the primacy of speech, that writing is a code for speech, and that language is descriptive rather than prescriptive.

Because of its importance, beginning reading instruction has drawn most attention and resulted in divergent viewpoints and concomitant controversies. It has been suggested that the most effective and efficient unit with which to begin instruction is the individual letter, the word, the sentence, the paragraph, or the story. For the most part, these alternatives have been offered by concerned and dedicated experts who are interested in providing the child with the most efficient, effective, and economical key to the world of reading.

Durr (5) reports that children with a deficiency in oral language would profit from a prereading program aimed at developing their verbal abilities before the children are introduced to reading. Many teachers and parents have been led to believe that technological advances, especially television, have produced a more sophisticated candidate for beginning reading instruction; however, at least one reading authority has suggested that linguists and psychologists see television interfering with the development of speaking and conversing. Other research findings indicate that attitudes and habits found in certain homes and communities during the preschool years may defeat all conventional methods of teaching the youngsters to read (6). Questions then arise concerning the extent to which the reading educators may expect to influence parents in raising their preschool children as well as questions concerning the nature of a prereading program.

## Picture Cues

Another issue which has provided consternation for the teachers of beginning reading, as well as the publishers of reading material, is the suggestion that pictures should be eliminated from beginning reading materials. Heilman (14) points out that neither the proponents nor critics of the use of pictures can point to empirical data for the support of his position.

Recent studies by Biemiller and Hartley provide some data, but the studies do not aid in the amelioration of the problem. Biemiller (3) suggests that the "use of picture cues and context may be ill advised" while Hartley (13) states, "Subjects presented the graphic stimulus plus a picture cue during study trials made the highest overall scores on the transfer test . . . ."

From a practical point of view, if the place to introduce the child to reading is the mother's lap, it would seem highly improbable that one could eliminate the picture book. As an integral part of the children's literature program, the picture book (which places equal emphasis on pictures and text) is and should be available at home, in preschools, and in first grade classrooms. Habits and attitudes formed early are most important to success in reading, and it would appear that statements regarding the elimination of picture cues should be examined carefully and at least qualified.

## Contextual Cues

The use of context cue is emphasized by many authorities and in a number of reading programs as a tool for the child to use in the decoding of the printed symbol—not without some basis for dissention and debate, however. The aforementioned article by Biemiller (3) questions the utilization of the context cue. On the other hand, Goodman (8) suggests that introducing new words out of context and before new stories are introduced may be unnecessary and undesirable. Barney (2) states that without context some words would have no pronunciation and meaning. The results of another recent investigation (13) indicate that a graphic stimulus plus a context cue were most successful when presented with a maximal contrast word list and that if graphic stimulus only is to be used, it is most successful with minimal contrast lists. Perhaps an implication can be drawn from an examination of either the Dolch Basic Sight Word List or the more recent Kucera-Nelson corpus which would reveal far more words of maximal contrast among the words most frequently used by children in either the thirties or the sixties (15).

## Word Identification

No other area in reading instruction has received the attention and stirred the emotions of both laymen and reading educators as has that of the so-called phonics versus sight-word controversy. The fact that in the actual teaching act the teacher utilizes elements of both approaches and that neither approach appears in pure form has done little to calm the situation.

At the present time, there are those who indicate that the approach to teaching reading must make use of the child's natural language. Thus, the language experience approach is suggested, but little mention is made as to how children are to learn phoneme-grapheme correspondence. Is it assumed that it is gained naturally without teaching?

To further confuse the teacher, she is referred to Chall's work (4) which suggests that an early emphasis on word identification skills will produce better readers than an approach which stresses whole words. Then the teacher is confronted with another viewpoint which suggests that Chall is wrong and that a balanced system which utilizes "visual, auditory, touch, and kinesthetic cues in combination and develops word identification and comprehension simultaneously, seems safer and is less likely to produce difficulties than any method which relies primarily on one sensory avenue . . ." (12). Word study skill must be emphasized and taught in a systematic way regardless of the particular approach to beginning reading instruction that is advocated. The teacher is responsible for deciding which emphasis to use with a child who does not respond to one approach. The child who has failed becomes the important entity in this situation, not the expert opinion nor the research findings which have resulted in the ambiguity of the meaningless debate among the decoding-meaning proponents.

As important as word identification is, a recent study provides no evidence which would support the contention that good identification is systematically related to good comprehension for all readers. Furthermore, the authors state that an approach which focuses upon word-by-word identification may "discourage the process of organizing input into the meaningful units which guide one in understanding what has been read" (16). Thus, specific attention must be given to developing comprehension.

## Comprehension

Comprehension or understanding is the pervasive goal of the reading process; reading without meaning is wasted time and effort. One would think, consequently, that investigation in the area would be overflowing, but such does not seem to be the case.

The terms "good comprehension" or "poor comprehension" are used so easily in describing youngsters who read at particular levels, just as if the terms were really communicating vital and specific information. Yet, when someone asks for clarification of the terms, it is difficult to avoid a circular definition and come up with specific referents which are meaningful. Comprehension, as it has been used and accepted, is a global term.

Even more condemning, however, is the fact that while there has been a growing emphasis on the development of inquiry, problem solving, and questioning, there is little to offer classroom teachers in terms of specific teaching strategies to help students expand their levels of cognitive thinking. Research has been conducted using Bloom's Taxonomy as a criterion for determining to what extent teachers are utilizing techniques to develop children's thinking beyond the literal level (1). The methodology utilized in most of these studies involves an analysis of the teacher's verbal behavior and is based on the assumption that questions teachers ask influence the levels of thinking of their students. Harris (11) states that research suggests teachers who tend to use a balance of questions attain better results than those who favor questions of one kind, whether they call for facts or interpretations, a specific answer or alternative responses. Studies by Schaftel and Guszak reveal that most questions asked by teachers could not be classified above literal level (1,10).

One of the difficulties in gathering data on the effectiveness of the cognitive aspects of teaching has been the difficulty of coding and categorizing teacher statements and questions. Popham and Baker (17) suggest that the utilization of a classification system distinguishing between higher and lower level goals would be of value to the teacher in establishing instructional goals. Smith (18) criticizes such an approach in describing people who recognize only two faces of comprehension, literal and inferential, or a larger group recognizing literal comprehension and critical reading. To remedy this situation, she has four models or categories of skills: 1) actual comprehension, 2) interpretation, 3) critical reading, and 4) creative reading. It would appear that research which facilitates the translation of the present theory concerning the development of thinking into operational classroom procedures has just begun.

## Summary

Research demonstrates that differences among teachers are more important than differences among approaches and materials in influencing children's levels of reading achievement. Other conclusions drawn from research focusing on specific areas of reading instruction have produced ambiguous and conflicting findings. If the results of the myriad of past and future investigations are to be of value, additional effort must be expended to provide the classroom teacher with information and experiences basic to the decisions he must make in implementing an effective reading program. The following suggestions are offered as possible steps for the amelioration of the problem.

1. Teachers must be involved in decisions relative to ongoing reading programs and especially to decisions relating to change and innovation. As a basis for these decisions, however, teachers must have an opportunity to become familiar with the newer programs and to be involved in their evaluations before adoption in the district. Criteria for assessing reading programs and materials should be made available to aid the teachers.

2. The teacher can and should assume responsibility for the evaluation of his own behavior and strategy in reading instruction. The utilization of videotape and less complicated forms of inter-action analysis would allow for the assessment of the effectiveness of specific lessons in terms of preset objectives. This procedure could be implemented in a formal inservice program or class, or informally within individual schools with the guidance of trained consultants.

3. Although the multidisciplinary approach to the study of reading is to be encouraged, some effort must be made to consolidate, clarify, and communicate significant findings to the classroom teacher. Reading educators, or perhaps professional organizations such as the International Reading Association, need to assume more active roles in providing the classroom teacher with objective analyses of reading research. Teachers as well as students need feedback, reinforcement, and meaningful criteria to guide their behaviors. The preparation of exemplary films, film loops, and video-tapes, which could be made available to groups or individuals interested in the latest information regarding reading instruction, might be accomplished through a cooperative effort between the International Reading Association and the Right to Read program.

4. Many authorities state that the upgrading of teacher education programs is basic to the improvement of student levels of reading achievement. Certainly this situation is true, but the responsibility must be extended beyond the campus. It is not possible to train teachers adequately in one or two reading methods courses with today's teacher mobility and his lack of knowledge about initial job placement, plus the particular approach to reading that he may find within a district. More emphasis must be placed on inservice training and an individual school district's responsibility to assimilate new teachers and to provide continuous education to its tenurial faculty.

This is an absolute necessity so that teachers understand the philosophy of reading instruction within the district. The teacher has a right to feel somewhat secure in that he has some local guidelines to direct his actions.

5. Generalizations which have been made about reading instruction in specific areas, such as word identification and comprehension, should be investigated to see if recommended practices and procedures work equally well with all teachers and all students. Such investigations might aid in the elimination of the verbalism which results from the use of gross generalizations and all-encompassing terminology and should help to clarify some of the apparent contradictions found in the literature today.

### References

1. Arnold, William, Nicholas Glaser, and Larry Ernst. *Teacher Move Analysis.* Dubuque, Iowa: Kendal/Hunt, 1971, 27.

2. Barney, LeRoy. "Linguistics Applied to the Elementary Classroom," *Reading Teacher*, 24 (December 1970), 221-226.

3. Biemiller, Andrew. "The Development of the Use of Graphic and Contextual Information as Children Learn to Read," *Reading Research Quarterly*, 6 (Fall 1970), 75-96.

4. Chall, Jeanne. *Learning to Read: The Great Debate.* New York: McGraw-Hill, 1967.

5. Durr, William K. "Reading Research and the Houghton Mifflin Readers," *Houghton Mifflin Reading Program*, Field Note E-949, September 18, 1970.

6. Gates, Arthur I. "Teaching Reading Tomorrow," *Reading Teacher*, 23 (December 1969), 231-238.

7. Gibson, Eleanor J. "The Ontogeny of Reading," *American Psychologist*, 25 (February 1970), 136-143.

8. Goodman, Kenneth S. "A Linguistic Study of Cues and Miscues in Reading," *Elementary English Journal*, 42 (October 1965), 639-644.

9. Guszak, Frank J. "Reading Comprehension Development as Viewed from the Standpoint of Teacher Questioning Strategies," EDRS ERIC MF A Report, 1968.

10. Guszak, Frank J. "Teacher Questioning and Reading," *Reading Teacher*, 21 (December 1967), 227-234.

11. Harris, Albert J. "The Effective Teacher of Reading," *Reading Teacher*, 23 (December 1969), 195-204.

12. Harris, Albert J. *How to Increase Reading Ability.* New York: David McKay, 1970, 78.

13. Harley, Ruth Norene. "Effects of List Types and Cues on the Learning of Word Lists," *Reading Research Quarterly*, 6 (Fall 1970), 97-121.

14. Heilman, Arthur W. *Phonics in Proper Perspective* (2nd ed.). Columbus, Ohio: Charles E. Merrill, 6, 96.

15. Johnson, Dale D. "The Dolch List Reexamined," *Reading Teacher*, 24 (February 1971), 449-457.

16. Oakan, Robert, Morton Weiner, and Ward Cromer. "Identification, Organization, and Reading Comprehension for Good and Poor Readers," *Journal of Educational Psychology*, 62 (February 1971), 71-78.

17. Popham, W. James, and Eva L. Baker. *Establishing Instructional Goals.* Englewood Cliffs, New Jersey: Prentice-Hall, 1970, 54.

18. Smith, Nila Banton. "The Many Faces of Reading Comprehension," *Reading Teacher*, 23 (December 1969), 249-259.

# REMEDIAL READING RESEARCH PROBLEMS

*Marciene S. Mattleman*
*Temple University*

*Barbara Rosenshine*
*Urbana, Illinois*

*Barak Rosenshine*
*University of Illinois at Urbana*

This paper presents reports of two intensive programs designed to improve the reading skills of low achieving pupils in innercity schools. Both projects were sponsored by Temple University and the School District of Philadelphia and were planned with two objectives: 1) to develop effective, portable, remedial instructional programs and 2) to enhance reading skills of sixth and fourth graders. The intention was also to create a model for the regular teachers in the schools who were offered demonstration lessons and materials to help with reading problems of their pupils.

In the first investigation, thirty sixth graders, whose IQ scores ranged from 80-100 and whose reading scores were below 3.0, were randomly assigned to experimental and control groups. The fifteen children in the treatment group came to a reading center one-half of each day while the controls remained in their classrooms. The large group was subdivided into three, with five children working with a teacher or teacher trainee, the latter being graded according to the achievement of his students. The common program was built around the *SRA Reading Lab 1A* with levels ranging from 1.2 to 3.0. Students were asked to do a stipulated number of cards daily, with the pace increasing as competencies developed. The SRA selections were analyzed so that the phonetic and structural skills taught in the readings were also stressed in the packets; e.g., if the recognition of the consonant blend *br* was emphasized in a SRA selection, exercises were found from existing sources or were made by the teachers to reinforce the same skill. These extra work sheets were inserted into the reading lab booklets so that the reading (eighty minutes) and word attack practice (thirty minutes) became a joint component. SRA's *Reading for Understanding* was utilized in teaching for inferences, and reading games were used (Quizmo, Phonics Rummy, etc.).

A token reinforcement system was devised in which students received points for persistency and accuracy as well as bonus points that could be turned in weekly for goods, such as comic books or models.

Pre- and posttesting included use of Metropolitan Achievement Tests (MAT) and Informal Reading Inventories (IRI). The raw gain scores were adjusted by analyses of covariance using pretest scores on the MAT and Iowa Test of Basic Skills (given to all children) as well as IQ scores as the covariates. The adjustment resulted in only minor changes on the posttest scores. For two groups, differences were significant at the .01 level on subtests of vocabulary and comprehension as well as on the IRI. Results on the MAT indicated a gain of nine months' growth after nine weeks of half-day instruction.

The second study was designed to replicate the pilot project, increasing instructional time to one academic year. The program was divided into three cycles, and changes were instituted on the basis of testing, staff judgment, and school scheduling. Random assignment to experimental and control groups was made of forty-eight fourth grade children, with IQ scores of 80-100 and reading levels of 2.0 or below. One teacher and three teacher trainees each taught three to six pupils. Individualized lessons were prepared from SRA Labs, Sullivan McGraw-Hill programed readers, SRA-BRS workbooks, games, and word analysis units compiled by the staff. Concept cards explaining difficult words and ideas were attached to each reading selection.

During the first cycle, points were awarded as token reinforcers and were exchanged for goods; the instructional sessions were 150 minutes long. In successive cycles, social reinforcement only was employed and the session time reduced to 60 minutes.

As in the pilot work, the MAT and IRI were used in pre- and posttesting. Differences between the mean scores of the experimental and control students were tested by analyses of covariance at the end of each cycle. In each analysis, IQ scores and appropriate pretest scores were used as covariates. Significant differences were obtained favoring the experimental group on the third cycle posttest (June) in reading ($p < .05$) and word knowledge ($p < .05$) as well as on the IRI scores in December ($p < .01$) and in June ($p < .01$). No significant differences were found on the MAT at the end of the first or second cycle.

Both studies were conducted by two of the three present investigators, one of whom was a faculty member in educational psychology and one in English education. With problems of retarded readers, it was believed that more than usual inputs were needed in dealing with a population that saw itself as a failure group.

Initial interest in the use of behavior modification techniques stemmed from success of this approach with exceptional populations (*1*). The writers believe it is necessary that children build a capacity to work for extended periods of time, to increase self-direction, and, at the same time, associate this productivity with a pleasant experience. When children learn at the "expected times," one can assume that learning is its own reward; when children see themselves as failures, they need an additional impetus to learn (i.e., tangible rewards). Within the confines of the centers, a token plan worked well; best results occurred when a point system was strictly adhered to. However, later experiences indicated that using token systems for whole class situations might be cumbersome and impractical. The writers would recommend, nevertheless, that activity areas with books, puzzles, comics, and teaching games be utilized as reinforcers for completed tasks—building up from short to longer goals in order to increase productivity. Social reinforcement has already been shown to positively affect achievement (*5*) and it is urged in heavy doses!

With regard to materials selection, Cohen (*2*) has already suggested some criteria. Are programs effective for specific populations? Are they adaptable for student self-direction? Are they easy for teachers to learn to use? In addition, the writers believe that other considerations are important for low achieving populations: 1) low level materials must not be too "childish;" 2) materials should be arranged as short term goals (whole books present too formidable a prospect); 3) programs should be such that parts can be easily deleted (e.g., if materials are unappealing or inappropriate, they should not be used for certain children); and 4) programs should provide immediate confirmation of response (e.g., autoinstructional).

Our greatest surprise in getting involved in school settings was the realization that, for low achievers, teachers were using materials that had already been associated with failure; that is, schools were greeting children in September with the same basal readers used in their classes the year before. At the moment, a search through the literature reveals the success of no one material over any other in itself; therefore, no one program is being specified. Whether the materials are traditional basal, programed, or linguistically oriented, they should be new to the children.

Regarding testing of reading abilities, the entire focus of any given journal or meeting could be involved with this topic with little resolution. Farr (*3*) has several excellent discussions regarding the values of various kinds of tests—formal and informal. For determining instructional level, Farr concludes that IRIs provide the most valid estimates. He also suggests using this measure as an ongoing tool for classroom diagnosis. In both projects cited, the latter practice was followed for the experimental groups (administrations at three week intervals), both to increase teachers' insights for preparing instructional sequences and to make the children more comfortable in test-taking situations. It might be argued that it was this practice that helped in reaching significant differences over control groups in posttesting.

Practice for standardized tests was also provided on an ongoing program component. When teachers were finished with the small instructional sequences (e.g., word analysis units), they prepared their criterion-referenced tests using the same formats as the standardized measures. In this way it was hoped that uncertainty concerning the test form would not be an impediment to achievement in posttesting. Whether this practice helped, we have no way of guaging; however, reactions from teachers after testing sessions indicate that behaviors consonant with anxieties were less frequent in experimental group testing sessions than with control groups. The variation between IRI and MAT scores was, as noted, quite large, corroborating Williams' findings (7) in which disabled readers showed large differences between performance on informal and standardized tests. Unlike other studies in which standardized test scores give a higher estimate of performance than IRIs (4), this was not the case here.

In both investigations, out-of-grade tests were utilized as evaluative measures. Realizing that a third grade score could be obtained by a sixth grade student by chance and that perhaps the child could read only on a first grade level (which could not be ascertained on a sixth grade test), tests were given that provided more information. Teachers graded tests themselves in order to diagnose problems initially and to evaluate teaching as the programs progressed. They were taught to do item analyses and to present plans to the investigators for using test data in individualizing instruction. It is the writers' contention that these procedures need to be implemented, regardless of class size, by supervisors making provision for time during the school day. Until teachers understand that pretesting, analysis, selection of a small instructional goal, and posttesting do enhance learning, the myriad of reading problems will probably not be substantially alleviated. Research shows that one gets what he teaches for (6); the necessity, therefore, of helping teachers in uses of tests for diagnosis is the crucial first step.

The authors' recommendations to those planning projects are offered with caution because of the realization that, despite the fact that experimental studies have been attempted, there were many uncontrolled variables. The following, however, should be of some value to those who anticipate operating centers for low achieving readers: 1) begin a program with short working periods and gradually lengthen them; 2) provide tangible reinforcements until pupils experience success in reading; 3) keep arrangements flexible to avoid being locked into schedules; 4) stagger the entrance of the groups, bringing in small numbers to learn procedures and become acclimated to individual pacing; 5) begin with short range, low level materials; and 6) utilize materials that provide the opportunity for self-checking.

Experience from these investigations leads one to conclude that it is more fruitful to work with upper graders in remediation than with younger children and that the older, perhaps more independent, child can monitor himself better. If the student is already at the third grade reading level, there are many autoinstructional materials from which to select. And at that level, despite his being a low achiever, the student has enough skills at his command to do some independent work.

Other difficulties facing university researchers who venture into schools may result from last-minute assemblies on testing days, student absences, teacher priorities, or problems with administrators, unions, and others. On the positive side, the researchers are in the "real world," face-to-face with reading problems, and may be a participant in effecting change in the behaviors and attitudes of both children and their teachers.

### References

1. Cohen, Harold L., James Filipczak, and John Bis. *Case I: An Initial Study of Contingencies Applicable to Special Education.* Silver Spring, Maryland: Educational Facility Press, 1967.

2. Cohen, S. Alan. *Teach Them All to Read.* New York: Random House, 1969.

3. Farr, Roger. *Reading: What Can be Measured?* Newark, Delaware: International Reading Association, 1969.

4. Glaser, N. A. "A Comparison of Specific Reading Skills of Advanced and Retarded Readers of Fifth Grade Reading Achievement," unpublished doctoral dissertation, University of Oregon, 1964.

5. Madsen, Charles, Jr., Wesley Becker, and Thomas Don. "Rules, Praise, and Ignoring: Elements of Elementary Classroom Control," *Journal of Applied Behavioral Analysis,* 1 (1968), 139-150.

6. Rosenshine, Barak, and Norma Furst. "Research in Teacher Performance Criteria," in B. O. Smith (Ed.), *Research in Teacher Education.* Englewood Cliffs, New Jersey: Prentice-Hall, 1971.

7. Williams, Joan L. "A Comparison of Standardized Reading Test Scores and Informal Reading Inventory Scores," unpublished doctoral dissertation, Southern Illinois University, 1963.

# SUCCESSFUL METHODS OF READING DIAGNOSIS

*John A. R. Wilson*
*University of California at Santa Barbara*

Successful reading diagnosis requires a criterion of success. The most obvious performance against which the evaluation can be made seems to be improved reading skill. Six approaches are discussed in this paper; major attention is focused on practices that can be used effectively by the classroom teacher.

## Hooked on Books

Fader and McNeil (2) have a global approach to the diagnosis of reading difficulties. Implicitly they assume that the basic problem is lack of motivation to read as far as the bulk of the poor readers from poverty backgrounds are concerned. The evidence they provide to support this diagnosis is impressive. When paperback books, magazines, and newspapers are used as the basis of instruction in all classes, when young people are provided with two books they can keep or trade plus a dictionary, and when the same young people are required to write at least two pages a week, even if the matter is copied, the average level of book reading increases from a prognosis of zero books per lifetime to a book every two days. Fader points out that not all of the boys and girls in the schools became readers, a factor which supports the position that the diagnosis of lack of motivation is incomplete. However, on the basis of improved reading performance that could be set in motion by a group of secondary school teachers, Fader's program deserves careful study.

## Sesame Street

Prevention of reading failure, particularly among the culturally different, is a major concern of reading teachers. Evidence is accumulating (9) that *Sesame Street* as a television show may provide the extra stimulation that children from poverty backgrounds need to become more competitive with middle-class children. The implied diagnosis that is fundamental to the program is that children from poverty will improve their reading if they are involved in learning the names and recognizing the shapes of letters, if they receive practice in hearing sentences organized according to the semantics of standard English, and if pleasure connections are tied into their learning experiences. It is too early to evaluate the effect on reading since the children affected by the program are still in the reading readiness stage, but the data developed by the Educational Testing Service seem to support the implied diagnosis. Reading will probably be improved if an increasing number of children are induced to watch the program systematically. Teachers can help spread the word through brothers and sisters who can take the idea home.

## Computer Diagnosis of Reading Tests

Geared to reading diagnosis, but still operating on a large scale, are the computerized diagnoses of test answers. Instructional prescriptions are made up for individuals who miss questions or groups of questions. *Metro '70 (3)*, by Harcourt, Brace, has this service for the upper age levels, and the California Test Bureau (a branch of McGraw-Hill) has the same service for the Comprehensive Tests of Basic Skills. The old Progressive Achievement Tests put out by the California Test Bureau provided diagnostic groupings on the front cover of the test booklet so that individual prescriptions could be written. The number of questions in each subcategory was too small to assure high validity or reliability in the diagnoses being made from the Progressive Achievement Tests. The same criticism can be made of the new tests of both companies, but busy teachers will almost certainly do a more skillful job of teaching to individual needs using the printouts than they do without any help of this kind. The computer has made individual analysis possible. Now all that is needed to have a superlative diagnostic tool is to have analyses based on longer and more complex tests.

## Kindergarten Evaluation of Learning Potential

Extended observation of individual children as they perform a substantial number of complex tasks under teacher guidance is probably the best way of obtaining the data needed for diagnosing probable reading success. In the Kindergarten Evaluation of Learning Potential (KELP), Wilson and Robeck (6) provide children with activities that both develop and measure the level of development of critical skills needed for beginning reading. The teacher keeps a record of the child's performance and modifies instruction as the needs emerge. As part of the KELP Summary Test Booklet, the performance over a year's time is analyzed to indicate children who have a good capacity to learn but may be weak on functional English usage, children who understand spoken English, and children who are competent in all skills including English expression. These materials have been used successfully with Indian children (5) and with other children in general (6).

It can be argued with a high level of validity that diagnosis should not be used in any of the circumstances so far enumerated. Many specialists would restrict reading diagnosis to activities that involve highly individual evaluation carried on by a skilled professional, probably a doctor of one kind or another. In this context, reading diagnosis would be limited to work done in reading clinics by reading clinicians. Certainly this kind of reading diagnosis should be considered in this paper.

## Types of Reading Disability

Robeck (7) described a diagnostic training program which enabled her students to make 79 percent accurate blind diagnoses from taped records of clinic children's oral reading. The reading passages were approximately 250 words in length and in the same format so that the readers would not be given cues about the difficulty of the materials. Only children who were average in intellect, who were not emotionally unstable, and who were not physically handicapped were used as subjects. Seven disabilities are described:

1. *Lack of Word Attack Skills*
   - Appears relaxed in the reading situation
   - Phrases well at times but lapses into word-by-word reading when recognition errors increase
   - Makes half the errors on word recognition
   - Makes substitutions more frequently than refusals
   - Uses substitutions either of like beginnings or of similar configurations that make sense in context
   - Makes refusals when no cue is available
   - Repeats when reading does not make sense
   - Tends to stop both before and after the substitution when a context clue to an unfamiliar word is needed
   - Having received phonetic training, tends to produce the first syllable and then wait for help

2. *Extreme Tension Related to Reading*
   - Marked change in tension symptoms when switched from talking to reading situation
   - Error ratio deteriorates rapidly once an error is made

- Compulsion to keep on reading

    *Some* stop after an error and continue without correcting

    *Some* stop after error and make multiple repetitions of parts of sentences they are sure of

- Proportion of errors is the same as for those who lack word attack skills but they are bunched differently

3. *Lack Motivation for Reading.* There are three subclasses within this general group.

    *Reluctant Reader*

    - Scores at or near grade placement
    - Reads well enough to do assignments but reads as little as possible
    - Is able to be self-directed when turned on—interest key

    *Careless Reader*

    - Poor reader but doesn't seem to care
    - No consistent error patterns
    - Makes errors on both easy and hard words; sometimes gets them correct
    - Up to a point, gets better in error ratio as reading gets harder but this falls off rapidly after a critical point

    *Hostile Overt Avoiders*

    - Tends to be expert at diversionary activity
    - Becomes overtly hostile when pressed to improve

4. *Overuse of Context*
    - Verbal ability exceeds decoding ability
    - Substitutions fit context rather than conform to word beginning or configuration patterns
    - Stops and corrects when meaning in the reading is lost
    - Makes rapid progress when decoding skills are taught

5. *Faulty Habits*
    - Picks up habits such as spelling out the word when learning on his own, a practice which later hinders progress
    - Does not attend to what he is reading orally
    - Lets his mind wander and keeps on reading
    - Continues moving lips and points when skill has become inefficient
    - Has other odd habits that interfere with reading

6. *Low Intellectual Ability*
    - Needs to be told the same thing many times
    - Has trouble learning readiness tasks
    - Makes low scores on IQ tests

7. *Nonreaders.* There are not many nonreaders even in reading clinics. Robeck reports 1 percent.

Classroom teachers as well as clinicians can use the categories developed by Robeck as a basis for remedial instruction.

## Neurological Dysfunctions

Rosner (8) objects to the use of the terms *dyslexia, minimal brain damage,* and *specific learning disability* as diagnostic terms in reading. Many remedial programs are structured to repair damage diagnosed as neurological dysfunction. In Figure 1, a flow chart is shown of the neurological input and output systems as they are related to reading. Consideration of the separate parts of this system may clarify ways in which problems can arise and the difficulty of interpreting the malfunction.

*Sensory Input.* A child receives input from the external world through the senses. For reading, the visual and auditory senses are particularly important although the other senses play a significant part in reading. Malfunctions can develop in the senses from a severity of total blindness or deafness to minor impairments that can be barely detected by an ophthalmologist or audiologist. Damage may be due to genetic causes or to environmental causes, including prenatal misfortunes (*11*).

*Sensory Integration.* Input from the different senses is integrated primarily in the reticular formation of the midbrain to produce what Penfield (4) calls the integration of the ongoing present which forms the basis of the experiential memory.

*Ideational Area.* In most people, the imagery from the integration of the ongoing present is fed into the right hemisphere where it is stored.

*Speech Area.* In most people, including about half of those who are left handed, speech patterns are stored in the same areas of the left hemisphere as are occupied by imagery in the right hemisphere. Connections run from ideation to speech and reverse. Sometimes these connections are damaged or badly formed.

*Voluntary Motor.* Output is initiated in the voluntary motor area which is situated along the fissure of Rolando.

*Muscular Motor.* Output is effected by the stimulation of the muscle systems that control the lips, tongue, eyes, or other systems.

The most common cause of damage is anoxia or oxygen starvation which causes neural cells to die. Damage can occur in any of the systems mentioned and in any of the connections between the

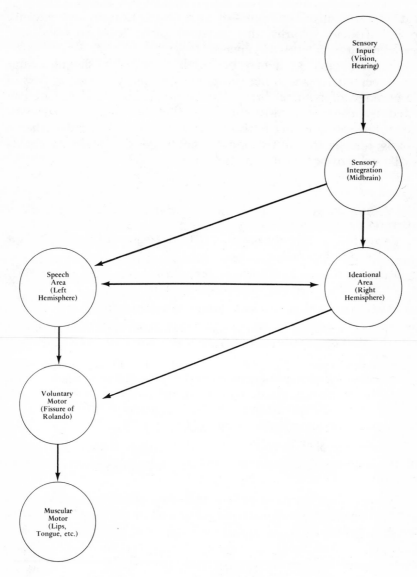

**Figure 1.** Neurological Flowchart from Sense Input to Muscle Response

systems. Most people suffer at least some impairment, often without measurable effect on their intellectual functioning. More clinic children suffer from neurological impairment than is proportionally true of the population as a whole; but most of the diagnosis of reading disability as being due to minimal brain damage is faulty. The effect of such a diagnosis is unfortunate since the teacher can hardly be held responsible for the results of physiological causes and may give up. In affluent suburbs, this diagnosis often leads to fraudulent treatments at high levels of expense (*10*).

Uncomfortable as it may be, teachers probably should assume that hyperactivity and other symptoms ordinarily classed as part of the etiology of minimal brain damage are learned and can be corrected by classroom instruction. Usually the kinds of diagnostic evaluations found earlier in this paper will be useful to the teacher as a basis for classroom treatment; the diagnosis "brain damaged" usually will not be useful to him.

### References

1. *Comprehensive Test of Basic Skills* (CTBS). Monterey, California: California Test Bureau, 1969.

2. Fader, D. N., and E. B. McNeil. *Hooked on Books: Program and Proof.* New York: Berkeley Medallion Books, 1968.

3. *Metro '70.* New York: Harcourt, Brace and World, 1970.

4. Penfield, W., and L. Roberts. *Speech and Brain Mechanisms.* Princeton, New Jersey: Princeton University Press, 1959.

5. Robeck, Mildred C. "The Use of the Kindergarten Evaluation of Learning Potential in Appraising the Capability of American Indian Children," paper given at California Educational Research Association, San Francisco, March 1970.

6. Robeck, Mildred C., and J. A. R. Wilson. *KELP Summary Test Booklet.* New York: McGraw-Hill, 1967.

7. Robeck, Mildred C., and J. A. R. Wilson. *Psychology of Reading: Foundations of Instruction.* New York: Wiley, 1972.

8. Rosner, S. L. "Word Games in Reading Diagnosis," *Reading Teacher,* 24 (January 1971), 331-335.

9. *Time, The Weekly Newsmagazine.* "Television," November 16, 1970, 70.

10. Van Donge, N. "Visual Problems in the Classroom," in J. A. R. Wilson (Ed.), *Diagnosis of Learning Difficulties.* New York: McGraw-Hill, 1971, 37-60.

11. Wilson, J. A. R. *Diagnosis of Learning Difficulties.* New York: McGraw-Hill, 1971.

12. Wilson, J. A. R., and Mildred C. Robeck. *Kindergarten Evaluation of Learning Potential (KELP).* New York: McGraw-Hill, 1967.

# PROBLEMS IN EVALUATING
# SCHOOL READING PROGRAMS

*Hugh I. Peck*
*Learning Institute of North Carolina*
*Durham, North Carolina*

Evaluation, as an educational specialty or discipline, has its roots in educational research and relies heavily on its personnel and its methodologies. Yet a distinction is needed, for research and evaluation are not the same tasks. The first problem is to separate reading evaluation from reading research. Glass (*3*) relates three distinctions that are meaningful to those who practice both research and evaluation:

1.  Evaluation attempts to assess the *worth* of a thing; research attempts to assess the scientific *truth* of a thing.
2.  Evaluation is that activity which seeks to directly assess *social utility*; research may yield such evidence but only indirectly.
3.  Research may be referred to as *conclusion-oriented* inquiry while *decision-oriented* inquiry typifies evaluation.

Accepting these distinctions, at least for the moment, those responsible for reading evaluations continue to face a multiplicity of problems. Though there is lack of theory and modeling for evaluation of programs, the deficit is not scarce enough to hinder an evaluator in his task. There are CIRCE models, Epic models, and EPIE and CIPP models—all of considerable flexibility and all of which have proven of value in given situations. Stanley and Campbell wrote the classic treatment on research design in Gage's *Handbook of Research in Teaching.* A good guess would be that a parallel treatment on evaluation is not far away. There is work to be done in the area of evaluation design; however, the placement of the need for evaluation design is not presented as a major priority. Glass's paper (*3*) moves in this direction.

Evaluators are not faced with a shortage of statistical methodology, computer technology, or capacity to handle complex statistical problems. If a shortage in this area exists, it is one of personnel with combined knowledge of educational problems and computer competency. Statistical methodology and computer competency and capacity are not the pressing needs. As the farmer said, "I'm not farming now as good as I know how." Evaluators are using the methodologies for handling data and statistical analysis in the same context.

There is one technical area that does provide real problems in evaluation—the area of tests and measurement. There is no need to recount the history of the measurement movement in education; it is well-known and not at issue. It was, however, based on the basic premise of differentiating among students and levels of students and of placing students on scales which were given various names. Items which did not distinguish the good from the poor student were deleted and other items inserted. Test demands of valuing and evaluation are greatly different. That 90 percent of the children should learn 90 percent of the concepts, as proposed by the criterion-referenced test group of Walbesser, Popham, and others, will not fit into the norm-referenced test mold. For the most part, evaluators have not mastered the use of criterion-referenced tests in their designs.

For example, when students on tests of paragraph meaning can answer the questions as well without reading the paragraphs as they do after reading the paragraphs (1971 study by Farr and Smith), we do have technical problems of tests and measurement in assessing reading program worth. Further, our ability to measure variables in the affective domain (1) is far outdistanced by our skills of measurement in the cognitive domain. We need concentrated effort to cross these hurdles. Yet there is a large and resourceful group—the test publishers—whose livelihood depends on providing evaluators with these instruments. Publishers are presently at work on the preparation of new instruments and the improvement of the existing ones. Available tests and measurement techniques are problems of significant proportion to reading program evaluators. Resources are, however, being expended toward a solution to this problem.

Stake (7) gives treatment to another of the major problems of evaluating reading programs:

> One of the things I like to see in an evaluation report is some indication
> of what is happening between teachers and students in the classroom,
> and for this purpose it seems to me very useful to have a classroom
> observation schedule .... I am saying today that we should gather
> observational data not because it leads to information about why the

kids are learning but because some audience needs to know what is going on in the classroom. Audiences have ideas about what is good and bad classroom activity. These are data that are fairly inexpensive to get. It takes a few hours to train a data-gatherer. How representative are the data gathered in a brief visit to the classroom? That is something to worry about, of course, but the worry should not prevent initial efforts to get such information. The evaluator studies the data and decides what more is needed. If the data turn out to be questionable the evaluator tells the audience what he found and why he does not find the finding credible.

Evaluators have not given the program's description—activities in the program—the attention it deserves. Replication is not possible without this information and responsibility for this rests on the shoulders of those of us who evaluate. The problem can and should be overcome. In addition, we should be careful in our reporting to address ourselves properly to the audiences for which our report is intended. The need is to address ourselves to those problems that are common to reading specialists or program directors and to evaluators. The first of these is a problem of mutual trust or faith (or at least for program personnel not to view evaluators as a threat). Granted it is difficult to separate the evaluation of programs from the evaluation of people. One of our more serious problems is the development of a mutual trust between those who direct or in some way are a part of reading programs and those who evaluate them.

A related problem has to do with clarifying or mutually agreeing, between programer and evaluator, on the role of evaluation in the determination of project or reading objectives. In the evaluation community, the role distinction is debated by Guba and Stufflebeam (8) on the one side and Glass and Scriven (3,5) on the other. Guba and Stufflebeam see a less active role for the evaluator in the establishment of objectives for the reading program. Oversimplied, they say, "Tell the evaluator your objectives in measurable terms, and we measure the distance you go in accomplishing them." Glass and Scriven, on the other hand, give the evaluator responsibility for "valuing" the objective before it is considered as a part of the project. Those of us in the evaluation of reading projects should face this problem and force a solution early in our deliberations.

Another problem that is faced jointly by evaluators and directors is that of data management and quality control. No project evaluation, no matter how brilliantly conceived and operated, is worth a grain of salt if input data are not carefully gathered and controlled before the program is analyzed. To the largest degree, evaluators depend upon those within a project to provide such data feedback. If the problem of mutual trust has not been faced, or if those in the project see no value in evaluation, the input data become highly suspect.

Education today recognizes the importance of accountability, and educators must address themselves to the problem. Educators have been told what accountability is and that it should be tied to evaluation; but they have been provided with little assistance in terms of methodology for combining education accountability and reading evaluation into a usable package. If those of us concerned with reading and evaluation do not work out the methodology, someone will sign a performance contract to do it for us. The solution to the problems surrounding reading, evaluation, and accountability is a joint responsibility of the evaluator and the reading project director and his staff.

The problems facing those concerned with the evaluation of reading programs might be placed into two classifications:

1. Technical problems (design, measurement, statistical analysis, data management, computer technology, and accountability).

2. People problems (mutual trust among evaluators and project personnel, agreement as to the roles and functions of each, and involvement of the teacher in a positive way in the evaluation).

So far, those of us who are concerned with reading and evaluation have raced far ahead in dealing with technical problems but have hesitatingly touched on those problems that are people oriented, those concerning the human element.

### References

1. Bloom, G. S. (Ed.). *Taxonomy of Educational Objectives: The Classification of Educational Goals,* Handbook 1. Cognitive domain. New York: McKay, 1956.

2. Bloom, Benjamin S., et al. *Handbook on Formative and Summative Evaluation of Student Learning.* New York: McGraw-Hill, 1971.

3. Glass, Gene V. "The Growth of Evaluation Methodology," mimeographed report, 1969.

4. Krathwohl, D. R., B. S. Bloom, and B. B. Masia. *Taxonomy of Education Objectives: The Classification of Educational Goals.* Handbook 2. Affective domain. New York: McKay, 1964.

5. Scriven, Michael. "The Methodology of Evaluation," *Perspectives of Curriculum Evaluation,* 1, AERA Monograph Series of Curriculum Evaluation. Chicago: Rand McNally, 1967.

6. Stake, Robert E. "The Countenance of Educational Evaluation," *Teachers College Record,* 1968 (1967), 523-540.

7. Stake, Robert E. "Evaluation Design, Instrumentation, Data Collection, and Analysis of Data," *Education Evaluation*. Columbus, Ohio: State Department of Education, 1969.

8. Stufflebeam, David L., et al. *Educational Evaluation and Decision Making,* Phi Delta Kappa National Study Commission on Evaluation, mimeographed, 1970.